PSYCHIC Pets

True accounts of animal
paranormal powers

PSYCHIC PETS

TRUE ACCOUNTS OF ANIMAL
PARANORMAL POWERS

MICHAEL STREETER

A QUARTO BOOK

First edition for the United States, its territories
and dependencies, and Canada, published in 2004
by Barron's Educational Series, Inc.

All inquiries to be addressed to:
Barron's Educational Series, Inc.
250 Wireless Boulevard
Hauppauge, NY 11788
http://www.barronseduc.com

Library of Congress Catalog Card Number
2003107786

ISBN 0-7641-2716-0

QUAR.PPET

Conceived, designed, and produced by
Quarto Publishing plc
The Old Brewery
6 Blundell Street
London N7 9BH

Project Editors: Fiona Robertson & Liz Pasfield
Art Editor: Anna Knight
Illustrator: Mark Duffin
Designer: Joelle Wheelwright
Assistant Art Director: Penny Cobb
Copy Editor: Jan Cutler
Proofreader: Anne Plume

Art Director: Moira Clinch
Publisher: Piers Spence

Manufactured by PICA Digital, Singapore
Printed by Midas International Printer, China
9 8 7 6 5 4 3 2 1

contents

3. saving lives

4. across the divide

5. seeing the future

INtRODUCtION

MOST OF US HAVE HAD SOME personal experience with pets. Many of us may have owned a cat, dog, guinea pig, rabbit, gerbil, hamster, or some other kind of pet when we were young. When we get older and set up our own homes, we often choose a cat or dog as a companion, or perhaps buy a pet for our own children. So we spend a great deal of our lives surrounded by animals and indeed, we may spend as much time with them as we do with our family or friends. We rightly value these animals for their friendship, love, and good company. But do we really understand them? Are we aware of their other remarkable qualities? It is very easy for us humans to take our pets for granted. Their love for us is unconditional and uncomplicated. But this very faithfulness and loyalty masks some remarkable qualities—qualities that run through the stories collected here in *Psychic Pets*.

How is it, for example, that our cat or dog knows we are coming home at a precise time? How can all kinds of animals— not only homing pigeons—find their way to people or places, sometimes over vast distances? And how can our pets be aware that we are in trouble and know what to do to help us? Most eerie of all, how are they able to keep in contact with us, even from beyond the grave?

STRANGE PHENOMENA

The origins of these phenomena are not explained by science. Indeed, mainstream science considers such questions beneath it, as not worthy of scientific investigation. Yet, if we take a new look at the animals that surround us, we will find plenty of stories that suggest such behavior occurs, even if it is unexplained. Most of us know of cats, dogs, or birds who seem to have the uncanny knack of anticipating exactly when their owners are coming home. They might be our own animals, or belong to people we know. The pattern is frequently similar: the pet begins to behave in an excited way some time before its owner arrives home. It does not seem to matter whether the person is home late or early, or whether he or she always comes home at irregular hours; the animal somehow seems to know. Usually the awareness shown by a pet is restricted to just one person: the human with whom they share a special, unseen bond. In one story, for example, a pet dog called Rusty always knew when his mistress was coming home, even though she was a flight attendant who flew on long- and short-haul flights and worked very irregular hours. The dog showed no similar signs of awareness toward the woman's sister, with whom he also lived. Another strange case is of the woman who decided to come home from a meeting and then changed her mind once she was in her car and returned to the meeting to speak to someone. Back home, her husband noticed that their pet cats, Flora and Maia, performed their usual welcoming antics for the woman's homecoming at precisely the time she initially decided to depart for home. There was no way that they could have heard her car; they had

simply reacted to what was going on in her mind at the time.

Does this suggest some kind of telepathy between pets and their owners? Can pets read our minds? One peculiar story suggests that pets may indeed do just that. British veterinarian Christopher Day reports the example of a dog named Betty, who was owned by his mother-in-law. Not only did this dog know when Christopher was on his way to visit, but she also knew *why* he was coming. If he was on duty as a veterinarian, Betty used to hide before he even came into the house. But if Christopher was merely making a social call, then Betty reacted with pleasure and awaited his arrival with excitement.

We can easily look for signs of telepathy in our own pets by observing their reaction to the imminent arrival of family members.

However, this
anticipation of an owner's arrival
is far from being the only
special quality that animals possess.
They also seem to understand when
something bad is happening to their owner,
wherever that person is. There are many tales of how
cats and dogs in particular have sensed the imminent
death of those they love. This often provokes howling,
whining, or meowing, perhaps in an effort to make their
family aware of what lies in store. In one chilling story, a
dog, Bob, whose master was away fighting in World War I,
spent much of one day underneath the bed, then later
began an uncharacteristic and blood-curdling howling. The
soldier's wife later discovered that her husband had been
killed at the precise moment the dog had started making
that terrible noise. The pet had apparently sensed during
the day that his master's life was drawing to an end, and
also had known the moment when death occurred.

CONTINUING DEVOTION

There are also well-documented cases of pets who have known that their
owners have died and have then escaped to keep a vigil over their graves,
even though they did not attend the funeral and the graveyards were
many miles from the family home. Such selfless devotion is indeed a
characteristic of our pets, although we may not always be aware
of it until it is too late. There is the well-known story of a
Japanese dog, called Hachi, who used to meet his master
after work every day at 5 P.M. at the local railroad station.

The man
sadly died at work,
but every day Hachi went back
to the station at precisely 5 P.M. in silent
tribute to his master. One of the greatest stories
of devotion by a pet is that of Greyfriars' Bobby, the
dog from Scotland who kept a lonely vigil by his master's
grave for more than 10 years, remaining there until his
own death.

The animals who show such devotion do not
have to be "pets" in the conventional sense. A strange
example involves that of a flock of geese. A Texan named
John Gambill had once saved a stricken goose on his
farm, and subsequently his land became a kind of
sanctuary for the wild birds. At the time of his death in a
hospital in Paris, Texas in 1962, a flock of geese flew over
the building and then circled it for some time, honking
their appreciation for the man who had befriended them.

The common theme of such stories is the relationship
that had developed between the animals and their human
friend. Sometimes though, animals can spontaneously
come to the rescue of humans with whom they have never
before had contact. The animal somehow senses that the
person is in distress and knows what to do.

WILD ANIMALS

A curious example of this selfless devotion happened in 1974 and involved a woman named Candelaria Villanueva, who was shipwrecked many miles off the coast of the Philippines. She related that a giant turtle swam underneath her tiring body and kept her afloat for many hours until sailors from a passing vessel rescued her. Oddly, Candelaria later recalled that another smaller turtle had swam beside her and that it had nipped her arm every time she began to fall asleep, thus averting the danger of her head falling beneath the water.

There are also clear accounts of dolphins coming to the rescue of humans. In 1996 British tourist Martin Richardson was scuba diving in the Red Sea when he was attacked and seriously injured by a shark. He was saved by three dolphins who drove the predator away.

HOMING ANIMALS

One of the most remarkable qualities displayed by pets is their ability to find their way back home to a person or a place over tremendous distances. There are dogs who have traveled across oceans, continents, and even battlefields to be reunited with their owner or with their home. How they manage to perform such feats is unclear; quite often dogs have managed to track down owners even when they have been far away in a place where the animal has never been before. Mere sense of direction, smell, or other physical clues alone cannot explain such occurrences. One case, for example, involved a dog called Prince crossing the English Channel and finding his master, who was a soldier, on a bloody battlefield in a country the dog had never visited before.

COMMUNICATING AFTER DEATH

Most moving of all, perhaps, are those stories in which pets and their owners have remained in communication even after death. These include the story of a dog, named Nigel who came back from the grave to rescue his mistress from attack late at night. Another is the truly remarkable story of an American veterinarian working in Africa, who became known as "Doctola," and whose life was saved by two dogs he had cared for as puppies. This last story is just one of the extraordinary true stories featured in *Psychic Pets*. These tales illuminate the bond that exists between our pets and ourselves, and they shine a light on the astonishing psychic awareness that so many animals seem to display.

As you read these stories from around the world, prepare to be moved and amazed. Consider also your own pets and the animals that shared your childhood. Chances are that, like the animals featured here, they too have remarkable psychic abilities of their own. If only we could know it.

chapter one
HOMING PETS

"THERE's no place like home," as the saying goes. This can also be true for pets. Many remarkable animals have refused to be parted either from the home they know or the family they love. Whether they have had to cross mountains, sail across oceans, or even walk through deadly battlefields, nothing can deter these brave and loyal pets. For them, the lure of home and their owners acts like a beacon drawing them back. No one yet knows how they can do it, but these stories of pets traveling home against all the odds are both moving and inspiring.

When Sugar was separated from the people he loved, the lovable cat was not going to let a mere 1,500 miles and a year-long journey across America get in the way of him and his family.

SUGAR,
the long-distance walker

SUGAR WAS A GOOD-NATURED CREAM-COLORED PERSIAN CAT who had been a loyal pet to the Woods family throughout the years. The family lived with Sugar in their home in Anderson, California. Sugar was in good shape, apart from a slight deformity of his left hip, which could be felt when he was stroked or petted. In fact, the problem with the left hip never seemed to bother him at all. The years went by, however, and sometime in the 1950s, old Mr. Woods decided it was time for him to retire. The family's retirement plans did not simply involve stopping work, but it included moving the family home, too. Mr. Woods had a dream of living on a farm in Oklahoma and had found just the place he wanted at Gage. The problem was: what to do about Sugar? Naturally the Woods family wanted the cat to go with them; he was after all very much a part of the family. There was one snag, however: Sugar hated traveling by car. Ever since they had owned him, Sugar had been scared of vehicles, and yet they were contemplating taking their beloved pet on a 1,500-mile trip by road to a new home. They did try, though. As they loaded their car on the day of their departure, Sugar was put inside ready for the long trek ahead. But as the family had privately feared, he had different ideas, and leapt out of the vehicle before it had even left the driveway. There was only one solution: the Woods family reluctantly gave Sugar to some friendly neighbors who said they would be pleased to offer Sugar a home. So the Woods family set off on the long journey to Oklahoma, excited about the new life ahead, but saddened that their little cat would not be a part of it.

A FRIENDLY STRAY

Nearly 14 months later, when Mr. and Mrs. Woods had settled comfortably into their new home, a stray cat turned up at their farm. The couple was delighted; they had not had another cat since Sugar and this stray was also cream-colored, and although it was a bit skinnier, it reminded them of the faithful pet they had left behind in California. Within a few days, the new cat was part of the family and readily allowed Mrs. Woods to stroke and pet it. It was then that she made the discovery. There, on its left hip, was a slight deformity. There could be no mistake: this cat did not simply just look like Sugar—it *was* Sugar. Quickly, the couple telephoned their former neighbors in Anderson to find out what had happened. They were told that just a few weeks after the Woods family had left California, Sugar was missing. The neighbors kept hoping he would turn up again, but he never did. Now, everyone knew why. This little cat had set off on the most incredible of journeys, battling through mountains, barren plains, rivers, and busy highways. Sugar had traveled for more than a year and walked nearly 1,500 miles to find a place he had never visited before. The reason? Sugar wanted to stay with the family he loved. As he lay purring on their floor, Mr. and Mrs. Woods knew that here was one cat that would not allow anything, not even half a continent, to come between him and his dearly loved family.

BORN IN 1921 Bobbie was of pedigree collie extraction, although there was a quarter part of old Scottish sheepdog in him, which meant he had a bobtail. Bobbie lived in Oregon with his owner, but in the summer of 1923 they took a vacation, driving east around Wolcott, Indiana, a town some 3,000 miles east of their home. It was here that disaster struck. Out of the window, Bobbie noticed various dogs from the town fighting. A tough kind of dog himself by nature, Bobbie decided he wanted a piece of the action and suddenly jumped through the open window to join in. Unfortunately for him, the town's proud dogs resented the intrusion of an outsider into their fight, and they all turned on the hapless collie. Together, the pack drove the fleeing Bobbie out of town, away from his owner and the safety of the car.

Bobbie's owner was distraught and drove around for some time in a desperate, but fruitless attempt to track his missing dog. For Bobbie, there was a more immediate problem: the pack of dogs on his trail was determined to hunt him down and teach him a lesson. Bobbie was no match for all these dogs combined, but he was a powerful and resourceful animal. One by one he was able to fight off his pursuers, until eventually he forced them all to give up the chase. After that, Bobbie's dilemma was a different one: how on earth was he to get home? By now his owner, although distraught, had given up any chance of seeing the hound again and was continuing his journey by a long, circuitous route that took in the north of Mexico. Pursuit of the car was impossible.

BOBBIE,
who was lost
on vacation

Bobbie was a resourceful dog who could not bear to be parted from his master; when he got lost on a trip he found his way home across 3,000 miles of mountains, rivers, and inhospitable terrain.

PSYCHIC INSIGHT

So, for Bobbie, there was only one thing to do, he would have to make his way back home on foot. According to well-documented accounts, for the next three and a half months Bobbie wandered across part of America, searching for his way home. Although he had traveled 1,000 miles he was actually only 200 miles nearer to his home.

Then, just like a light bulb switching on in his head, the way home came to him in a psychic flash. Although Bobbie had been rounded up as a stray and put in a truck with other dogs, he escaped and shot off like an arrow in the right direction—due west. From that moment on, even though he was thousands of miles from home and in a strange environment, Bobbie was unerring in his direction. In one stretch alone he was said to have covered almost 500 miles in just one week heading toward Denver. Bobbie's route took him across the Rocky Mountains in winter, across wide, bitterly cold rivers, and through inhospitable terrain. On one occasion, the determined collie had leapt from a river bridge to escape capture. Eventually, exhausted and thin but otherwise well, Bobbie arrived at the home of his astonished owner in Oregon, six months after he had been feared lost forever. Throughout all his hardships—the fights, the hunger, and the cold—Bobbie had never forgotten the one thing he craved more than anything: the irresistible lure of home.

Beethoven was an unusual name for an unusually clever dog. Separated from his owners on holiday, he trekked through ice and snow to make it back to the family and house he adored after months of hard and dangerous effort.

aVIGNON, FRANCE HAS BEEN THE SETTING for some unusual stories about animals. The first one takes place in 1970 when a building worker, Jean-Marie Valembois, left his home in northeast France to seek work close to Avignon. Sadly for Jean-Marie, the journey meant he had to leave his faithful two-year-old sheepdog, Black, with a cousin. Some months later, however, there were reports of a stray dog around the building site where Jean-Marie worked. The dog's description seemed familiar, but Jean-Marie wouldn't dare let his hopes get too high. But as soon as he saw the "stray," there was no doubt that the animal was none other than his sheepdog, Black. The dog nearly knocked over his master with his exuberant greeting, such was his delight at being reunited. Black had walked 500 miles to an unknown area simply to be with the master he adored. Needless to say, they were never apart again.

The extraordinary story of Beethoven, a white spitz, also took place in Avignon. It was August 1998, and this handsome, five-year-old dog was

BEETHOVEN
braves the snow

staying with his French family, who were enjoying a break in Avignon during the traditional season for French vacations. Soon, however, August was drawing to a close and it was time for the family to return to their home far up in the northeast of France, close to the French–German border at Nomeny in the province of Lorraine. There was just one small problem: there was no sign of Beethoven.

LAST WALK

The high-spirited Beethoven had given his owners the slip while out for a last walk, and he was nowhere to be seen. The distraught family delayed their departure for as long as they could while they waited for Beethoven to appear. Finally they could wait no longer—they had work and college to return to—and so they left Avignon.

The heat of summer gave way to one of the coldest winters France had experienced in recent years: the rivers and lakes froze, and the snows fell. Beethoven's owners continued to mourn his loss, certain that the harshness of the winter spelled doom for their dog's chances of survival. However, they had not counted on Beethoven's indomitable will. From accounts, it seems that as soon as he got lost, Beethoven had become disoriented by his unfamiliar surroundings. He headed for the only place he knew he could find: the family home 500 miles away back in northeast France. Day after day, Beethoven padded through first the heat, and then the rain, and later the snow. Finally, one day in March of the following year, Beethoven arrived at his home, having walked from the Mediterranean all the way to the border with Germany. When he arrived home he was hungry and thin. But as his overjoyed owners put it, Beethoven was full of *joie de vivre* just to be at the place he had sought for many a long month.

T HREE-YEAR-OLD PERSIAN, HOWIE was a cat who enjoyed the good things in life: the best food, a comfortable house, and lots of fuss and attention. His owner, 15-year-old Kirsten Hicks from Adelaide, Australia, doted on the cat, and Howie was clearly very fond of his mistress. Outside of school, the pair were practically inseparable. In 1977, however, the Hicks family was getting ready for a long overseas trip. Kirsten was looking forward to the trip, but was concerned about what to do with Howie while she and the rest of the family were away.

HOWIE,
who walked home across Australia

Howie the Persian cat looked an unlikely hero, but he was tough enough to make his way across hundreds of miles of snake-infested, perilous land.

Obviously they could not take the Persian with them on this journey, but Kirsten did not trust anyone outside her family to look after her precious pet. In the end, Kirsten came up with a solution: could Howie stay with Kirsten's grandparents, who loved the cat almost as much as she did? Although her grandparents lived more than 1,000 miles away on the Gold Coast of Queensland, Kirsten was adamant that this was the answer, and so the arrangements were made. Kirsten bade Howie a tearful farewell and her grandparents assured her that the cat would be just fine with them.

A month later, Kirsten and her family returned to Australia after their trip and headed first for Queensland to collect Howie. Kirsten's grandparents, however, had some bad news to tell their granddaughter. They had not told Kirsten while she was away because they did not want to ruin her trip, but Howie was missing. They assured her that they had done all they could to find the cat, but to no avail. He had simply vanished. Kirsten was understandably shocked by the news, and although she did not blame her grandparents, whom she knew also loved Howie, she went back to her home in Adelaide with a heavy heart. Her parents tried to console her with the offer of another cat to replace Howie, but Kirsten rejected this. For her, no cat could replace her lovely Persian pet.

ALL ALONE

All Kirsten could think about was Howie, an animal who enjoyed his comforts, lost and alone in a strange environment. She felt sure Howie could not survive for very long on his own.

The months passed, and soon it was a year since Howie had vanished. One day while Kirsten was at school, a dirty, scrawny cat turned up at the family home. Mrs. Hicks instantly took pity on the poor creature who was ravenously hungry, bleeding, and pitifully thin. The cat gratefully gobbled down some tuna Mrs. Hicks gave it, and then a thought struck her. Maybe Kirsten would like to look after this needy pet, as a replacement for poor old Howie. So she took the cat inside and waited till Kirsten came home. The teenager took one look at the thin, bedraggled animal and shouted in excitement: "Howie!" Mrs. Hicks was stunned, but then she examined the cat more closely. Underneath the grime and the dirt, was the unmistakable fur of a Persian cat. And from its reaction to Kirsten, it was quite clear who this cat was. Howie had made it home. Somehow, this well-fed and cosseted cat had traveled more than 1,000 miles from Queensland, across mountains, barren plains, and rivers, braving all sorts of perils, from dogs to snakes, scorpions, and other wild animals. Now, despite all his hardships, Howie could enjoy the comforts of his Adelaide home once more.

TRAVELING BY TRAIN CAN SOMETIMES be a confusing business. Large and busy railroad stations can be bewildering places, particularly in unfamiliar countries. It is not always easy to know which is the right train to board, but for animals it is surely impossible. Yet, there are always exceptions to any rule. And the exception in this case is a bull terrier by the name of Peter. This extraordinary dog not only knew the inner workings of the railway system of an entire country, but he also used this knowledge to track down his master, who he believed was missing.

The story began in Egypt one day in 1901. Mr. Jobson was an official in the British government's colonial service. He had been stationed for some time in what was then called Upper Egypt, up the river Nile and deep into the heart of the country. He was accustomed to taking the train north to Cairo for business trips, a journey that could take

PeteR's
train journey

Peter the intrepid bull terrier knew just what to do when his master left on a business trip — he hopped on a train and set off in hot pursuit of him.

as long as 15 hours. Mr. Jobson usually was accompanied by his faithful bull terrier, Peter, on these journeys. The pair would travel in the first-class section, with Mr. Jobson doing a crossword puzzle or reading some paperwork, while Peter sat quietly at his feet, not even looking out of the window at the passing countryside. These trips were a regular feature of the pair's lives. Recently, however, Mr. Jobson had been transferred to a new position in Damanhur, near Alexandria, which lies on the opposite side of Cairo from Upper Egypt. Once again Mr. Jobson would use the train to take them to any business engagements south to Cairo. This time the trip would take a mere three hours.

A DETERMINED PET

One day, Mr. Jobson received an urgent message requesting his immediate presence in Cairo. He considered whether he should take his usual traveling companion with him to the capital, but he thought that because of the urgency of the

meeting and the unpredictability of his trip, it might be best to leave Peter behind this time. Accordingly, Mr. Jobson left Peter in the care of a friend who lived nearby, and hurried off to catch his train to Cairo.

Peter had many virtues as a dog and as a pet, but patience and quiet acceptance were not among them. The animal was distinctly unhappy at being left behind and could not understand why his master was going without him, or where. According to his canine reasoning there was only one thing to do: Peter had to follow his master, who had surely left him behind by mistake. So the bull terrier escaped from the confines of his temporary home, and trotted down to the obvious place to start his search: the train station at Damanhur. Here the animal found the right platform and then boarded the express train bound for the capital. Once he had arrived at the bustle of the Cairo railway station, Peter pondered his next move. Surely his master must have gone back up country to their old

lodgings in Upper Egypt? So the bull terrier padded his way to the correct platform, then sat down and waited for the train to Upper Egypt, which was not due to arrive for three hours. Once on the train, Peter took his natural position in the first class compartment and settled down for the 15–hour trip ahead.

No one bothered him on his journey; the fierce-looking bull terrier was not a dog many people thought to be playful. In any case, to passengers and ticket inspectors alike, Peter looked like a dog who knew where he was going. Once in Upper Egypt, Peter quickly made his way to the old house where he and his master had stayed. To his surprise, Peter could find no sign of Mr. Jobson, just some of the staff who had worked with him in the past. Dismayed, but undeterred, Peter now hit upon another plan: his master had surely stayed in Cairo after all. So with little further waiting, he trotted back to the station, went to the correct platform, and boarded the next train back to the capital. Fifteen hours later, Peter leapt off the train and began searching for his master's friends in Cairo in the hope that Mr. Jobson was visiting one of them.

DOGGEDNESS REWARDED

One by one Peter went to the friends' homes, but still there was no sign of Mr. Jobson. One friend however, recognized the familiar animal, and tried

Peter made an excellent first class passenger and was clearly a dog who knew where he was going.

to shut Peter in a room while he contacted Mr. Jobson for advice. Peter, however, would have none of this. He swiftly escaped, and once again made his way back to the railway station in Cairo. All was becoming clear to the bull terrier: his master must have made his way back home to Damanhur. So Peter found the correct platform and, after a brief wait, he boarded the next express train north to his new home. On arriving in Damanhur, Peter waited patiently until a first-class passenger opened the train door and he jumped down with some dignity on to the platform. The animal was now, of course, back where he had started some 42 hours ago. This time his perseverance was rewarded: back in Damanhur he found his master, Mr. Jobson, patiently waiting for him. One of the friends who had seen Peter in Cairo had contacted Mr. Jobson to alert him to the dog's whereabouts, and the official was not overly surprised to see Peter calmly returning home by train. Not only

had the entire journey taken nearly two days but it also had involved four different train journeys and three different railway stations. Somehow Peter had managed to find his way unerringly across half of Egypt by train, and was then able to find his way safely back home. His ingenuity and ability made him a very special dog. But what really made Peter outstanding was his incredible loyalty to his master; mere distance was no obstacle to reuniting himself with the person who meant more to him than anyone else in the world.

PRINCE braves the battlefields

JIMMY BROWN, FROM IRELAND, joined the British army when World War I broke out in 1914. He decided to move his wife, Colleen, and dog, Prince, to a house in Hammersmith, West London, which would make it easier for him to see them when he had some leave from the fighting in France. Jimmy's regiment was one of the first to get involved in the early skirmishes and naturally, both Colleen and Prince, who doted on his master, missed him while he was away in battle. After some time, though, Jimmy was given a short period of leave, which he gratefully spent in London. Far too soon, however, the time came for Jimmy to return to the front, and this time Prince seemed particularly upset by his master's departure. Indeed, for three days the usually hearty animal refused to eat any food. He was listless and moped around in a thoroughly dejected way. Then, just as Colleen thought Prince's behavior couldn't get any worse, he disappeared. The dog's disappearance was a worry to Colleen. She knew what dreadful hardships Jimmy was enduring on the battlefield, and that the thought of his dog's friendship and companionship had helped keep him going. Now, that faithful friend and companion had vanished.

Only Prince knew how he did it but somehow the dog crossed foreign land and sea to be with his adored master once more.

For 10 days Colleen hunted high and low for the dog, but he was nowhere to be seen. Finally, she realized she could put off the inevitable no longer. Although it would make his already hard existence even harder, she would have to tell Jimmy. And so, with a despondent heart, Colleen wrote to Jimmy in France explaining that although she had looked everywhere, his precious dog Prince had disappeared. Jimmy might, she hoped, take some comfort from the fact that Prince's behavior and refusal of food were testimony to the pet's devotion to his master.

AN INCREDIBLE JOURNEY

When Jimmy received Colleen's sad letter in his trench at Armentières, he couldn't hide a wry smile. For there, at his feet, watching him as he read his wife's letter was none other than Prince himself. Somehow, in a way that Jimmy could only begin to imagine, the little dog had made one of the most incredible journeys any animal has ever attempted.

Prince first must have left his new home in West London and then walked the 70 or so miles to the English Channel. Then, given that the collie-terrier mix hardly could have swam the Channel, he must have smuggled himself on board a ship taking supplies or troops to the war. Once in France, however, Prince's troubles were far from over. The French coast was some 60 miles away from where Jimmy was fighting, and much of the journey was through war torn and dangerous countryside. Battles were in full cry, bullets were flying, shells were exploding—some filled with deadly gas. Yet, Prince found his way through the blood and mud of the countryside to pick out Jimmy from 500,000 other British troops on the front line. No wonder Jimmy could hardly believe his eyes when the muddy little dog appeared in his trench, or that a relieved Colleen gasped in astonishment when she received the news from Jimmy. But the evidence was before Jimmy's eyes: the faithful dog had defied the horrors of war to track down his missing master.

BORDER COLLIES ARE ACUTELY INTELLIGENT and sharp dogs that are often trained by farmers to round up the sheep, and they are a familiar sight in the hills and valleys of rural Wales while they are at work. One of these expert sheepdogs was Pero, a black-and-white border collie who lived on a farm near Porthmadog in Wales. Now 10 years old, Pero was a veteran sheepdog as well as something of a family favorite, and the Pugh family was understandably very proud of him. Despite his advanced years, Pero had lost none of his sense of

PERO
finds a familiar face

adventure and exploration, but unfortunately this trait could sometimes get him into trouble. One such occasion was in 1985. It was the end of a normal day on the farm when Gwen Pugh and her son Tudur suddenly realized that the familiar figure of Pero was not anywhere to be seen. Mrs. Pugh thought about where the dog may have gone, and then it occurred to her what might have happened. That afternoon a truck had delivered calves to the farm, and Pero had been around at the time. Mrs. Pugh and her son soon realized they hadn't seen Pero since then. The ever-curious sheepdog must have sniffed around inside the truck, only to be shut up inside, and driven away. A quick telephone call confirmed that Pero was, indeed, with the haulage company at its headquarters. The only snag was that this was some 100 miles away, near Carmarthen in South Wales. The haulage company driver kindly offered to meet Mrs. Pugh the next day halfway between the two at a market, to hand over the errant Pero. But before Mrs. Pugh even had time to leave her farm, the boss of the haulage company was back on the phone with bad news: Pero had vanished again, but this time no one knew where he was.

A NEEDLE IN A HAYSTACK

Determined to find their much-loved sheepdog, the Pugh family contacted the local police in the area where he was last

When Pero's adventure left him stranded he didn't panic. The old sheepdog used his expert skills to find a familiar face.

seen, and the Royal Society for the Prevention of Cruelty to Animals, in case he had been handed in by a member of the public. They even broadcast messages to the public via local radio. But it was of no use. Pero had vanished into unfamiliar territory more than a hundred miles from home. As Tudur put it, it was like looking for a needle in a haystack. A week passed and the Pughs were beginning to reconcile themselves to the fact that they would never see the mischievous old sheepdog again.

Then it happened. Mrs. Pugh's daughter, Sian Evans, was staying at her husband's family home at Burry Port, about 15 miles south of Carmarthen where Pero was lost, and in the opposite direction from Porthmadog. One evening, she noticed a dog that looked familiar

walking nearby. To her utter astonishment it was Pero, the old black-and-white sheepdog she used to know back on the farm. The tired old dog, drawing on every ounce of resource, instinct, and ability he possessed, had somehow found his way to a strange house in a strange town in an area he had never visited before and made it safely to a person he knew.

Exactly how Pero found her remains a mystery to this day, but to Gwen Pugh and her son Tudur, this did not matter; all they cared about was that their beloved sheepdog had made it back to safety against all the odds.

To Joker the spaniel, his master's departure across the Pacific Ocean to fight in the war was no laughing matter; so the clever dog simply jumped on a ship and followed him, until he was reunited with the astonished officer.

SOMETIMES A PET'S NAME seems to suit the character of the animal perfectly, but there are occasions when the name gives little clue to its true nature. So it was with a cocker spaniel named Joker. Although the dog was certainly a playful soul, the name Joker hardly described the resourcefulness and bravery that this little dog was to display to stay with his master. The story began during World War II when Joker's owner, Stanley C. Raye, was serving as an army captain. One day Captain Raye, who lived in Pittsburg, California, received orders that he was to leave on a mission to an undisclosed destination in the South Pacific. No one in the family, not even the Captain himself, knew exactly where he was heading. Naturally, his friends and relatives were concerned about his impending departure and his safety, and his playful companion, Joker, was affected, too. Indeed, for two weeks after Stanley set off on his secret mission, the spaniel ate little and was generally very glum. Then one day Joker disappeared from the family home. The dog's precise movements immediately after leaving home are not known. But some days later the spaniel was seen by two army medics at Oakland, some 30 miles from the Raye home and from where many naval ships set sail. Joker evaded capture and then did something extraordinary: he jumped on board one of the many army transport ships that was bound for the South Pacific.

JOKER
crosses the Pacific

JOYFUL REUNION

The spaniel had never even been on board a ship before. Yet, here he was, aboard a vessel, steaming out into the expanses of the Pacific Ocean. Joker's story could have ended there; stowaway dogs were regarded as a nuisance in the cauldron of war, and the ship's commander was only deterred from dispatching Joker when an army major took pity on the lovable spaniel and promised to look after him. And so the vessel moved out into the ocean, stopping here and there at various islands to pick up supplies or offload troops. At each different island Joker would show initial interest in his new surroundings and then remain calmly on board the ship—that is, until Joker's vessel reached one particular island, when the spaniel suddenly reacted very differently. His ears pricked up and then, his nose sniffing the air, Joker bolted for the gangway and dry land. The major who had saved Joker ran ashore after him, only to find the dog dancing delightedly at the feet of a bemused-looking army captain. Seeing the major's look of surprise, the captain quickly explained who he was. His name was Captain Stanley C. Raye, and he was Joker's owner. At first neither man could quite take in what had happened; in the chaos of Oakland, Joker had somehow managed to get on board the right ship heading for the right island to reunite him with his beloved master.

Stubby's
thousand-mile
adventure

T O MANY, STUBBY may not have seemed a particularly special animal. With his short, stubby legs, undistinguished muddy-brown coat and average size, Stubby looked the very image of an ordinary, crossbred dog. But to Della Shaw, Stubby was a very special animal indeed.

Della, from Colorado Springs, Colorado, had been disabled and mute since birth. For her, Stubby was a loving friend, a fun companion, and a constant source of joy in her life. Best of all, he was dependable and always there when she needed him to cheer her up. All of which made it even harder for Della to bear one day in 1948 when Stubby was missing.

It happened when Della and her grandmother, Mrs. McKinzie, had been on a lengthy stay with relatives in Indianapolis, more than 1,000 miles away. Soon after they started home in their truck, Stubby vanished. No one knew how it happened, although everyone assumed that the dog had fallen out of the truck. Mrs. McKinzie wasn't even totally sure *where* it had happened, though she suspected it was somewhere on the Illinois–Indiana border. Whatever the cause and the place, Della was distraught at the loss of her great friend and companion. It felt as if a piece of herself had been ripped away.

Stubby knew that his young mistress Della relied on him for love and friendship, so when the little dog got lost in the middle of America, he knew he had to make it home.

Della's grandfather, Harry McKinzie, and his wife did all they could to track down the little dog, knowing how much he meant to their beloved granddaughter. They placed ads in local newspapers along the route the truck had taken, and enlisted the help of family and friends in a search. Sadly, none of this helped to find Stubby.

DWINDLING HOPE

As the days turned into weeks and then months, the family realized that the chances of seeing Stubby again were dwindling fast. The first anniversary of Stubby's disappearance came and went, and still there was no news. Della never forgot her great friend, but slowly came to terms that he was no longer part of her life. Besides, she had recently moved home with her grandparents, and so there was plenty to occupy her thoughts.

One spring day in 1950, Mr. McKinzie went for a long walk and by chance, passed by their old home. An experienced and worldly man, Harry McKinzie could cope with most things life put his way, but even he was taken aback by what he now saw. There, on the sidewalk next to their old house, sat the disheveled and bleeding, but unmistakable figure of Stubby.

The dog was sitting calmly as if waiting for something or someone. He barely acknowledged Mr. McKinzie, but when he was taken back to their new home he simply yelped with joy when he saw Della. As for the teenager, she cried tears of relief as she hugged the bruised and hungry little dog, overjoyed that her prayers finally had been answered. As the family had suspected all along, this was no ordinary dog. His special bond of love and friendship with Della could not be broken by mere distance. Although it had taken nearly 18 months and 1,000 miles, Stubby had been determined to get back to the person he loved. And although she could not speak the words, the joy now beaming from Della's face told the world how much Stubby's loyalty and love meant to her.

THE FAMOUS AUSTRALIAN KELPIE is a breed of dog developed in the nineteenth century to cope with that country's rising sheep population and its often harsh, hot climate. As well as being tough and hardworking, the kelpie is also known for its cunning. This may be because it is believed that the breed might have been crossed with the native wild dog of Australia, the dingo. Whether this is true or not, the kelpie is certainly a resourceful animal, as demonstrated by a dog named Sweep who lived in Western Australia in the 1920s.

Sweep was a typical black-and-tan-colored kelpie who worked on a farm. Besides working with sheep, Sweep was also a constant companion to his master, accompanying him around the farm and on any local visits he made. This farmer used to make fairly regular trips into his local town. The town, however, lay across a stretch of water and was reached by ferry. The cost of the ride was a penny, and this was charged both to humans

SWEEP'S
ingenious way of paying a fare

When Sweep was separated from his master by the price of a ferry fare, the dog knew what he needed to do: find someone who would buy his ticket for him.

and to any animals traveling with them. So it was that Sweep and his master used to cross into town, paying a penny each time for the river ferry.

One day when they were in the settlement, Sweep became separated from his master. While the dog made a frantic search in the town for his owner, the farmer made his way back home as usual. Eventually, Sweep realized his master was no longer around, and so he too, decided to set off for the farm, and made his way to the ferry as usual. There was, however, one small problem. Sweep had no money for the ferry crossing. Three times the kelpie tried to get on board the small ferry, but each time the ferryman blocked his path.

NO MONEY, NO RIDE

The rule was simple whether you were a human or a dog: no money, no ferry ride. The dog's plight appeared hopeless, but Sweep was not to be beaten. With a knowing look, the black-and-tan animal trotted back into the town. Here the experienced sheepdog "rounded up" one of his master's friends, making it perfectly clear that the man was supposed to come with him. So the man followed Sweep until they

came to the ferry crossing. Both the friend and the ferry toll man were baffled until Sweep made it clear what was supposed to happen next, by moving quickly from one man to the next. Both men suddenly understood; it seemed the friend was being "persuaded" to hand over Sweep's fare to the ferryman. Both men looked at each other and laughed, but there was no other explanation. From Sweep's insistent manner, the friend did not have any choice. He duly handed over the penny fare and Sweep trotted on to the ferry. Soon Sweep was back home on the farm and reunited with his master. The dog's astonishing behavior became the talk of the town for months, but for Sweep, the matter was quite simple: nothing, not even a ferry fare, would come between him and his master.

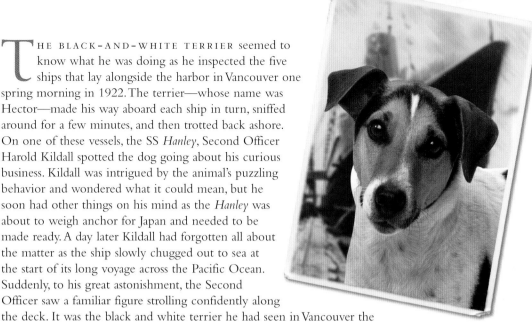

THE BLACK-AND-WHITE TERRIER seemed to know what he was doing as he inspected the five ships that lay alongside the harbor in Vancouver one spring morning in 1922. The terrier—whose name was Hector—made his way aboard each ship in turn, sniffed around for a few minutes, and then trotted back ashore. On one of these vessels, the SS *Hanley*, Second Officer Harold Kildall spotted the dog going about his curious business. Kildall was intrigued by the animal's puzzling behavior and wondered what it could mean, but he soon had other things on his mind as the *Hanley* was about to weigh anchor for Japan and needed to be made ready. A day later Kildall had forgotten all about the matter as the ship slowly chugged out to sea at the start of its long voyage across the Pacific Ocean. Suddenly, to his great astonishment, the Second Officer saw a familiar figure strolling confidently along the deck. It was the black and white terrier he had seen in Vancouver the

Hector
homes in

day before. Kildall was surprised and puzzled. He had seen the terrier "inspecting" all five ships in Vancouver—why had he chosen this one? And what was to become of this canine

Having discovered his master was an ocean away, Hector the terrier didn't panic, but calmly found the next ship going in the same direction.

SS Hanle

?

stowaway? Fortunately, the skipper of the vessel liked dogs as much as Second Officer Kildall and agreed to accept Hector's presence aboard. Soon the animal settled into the voyage and became a familiar and even valued member of the crew. Most nights he would faithfully keep watch with Second Officer Kildall, to whom he had formed a special attachment.

JOURNEY'S END

Eventually, the *Hanley* completed its long haul across the Pacific and made anchor at Yokohama Bay in Japan. It was then that Hector's behavior began to change. During the voyage the terrier had been calm, almost placid, as if he did not have a care in the world; now he became anxious and restless, and began pacing up and down the deck. The object of his concern seemed to be another ship at anchor nearby. The SS *Simaloer*, a Dutch-registered vessel, was also carrying a load of timber, but clearly had arrived in Japan a few days before the *Hanley*. Kildall— who was puzzled by the dog's apparent distress—watched as a small boat left the *Simaloer* and headed for the port landing area. As the little boat drew closer to the *Hanley*, Hector became more and more agitated, jumping and barking in a most unfamiliar way. Just as it seemed that

the terrier was going to leap into the harbor in his excitement, a man down in the small boat waved his arms and shouted the dog's name. To Kildall's astonishment, the stranger in the boat knew who the animal was—his own pet terrier. Within a few minutes, William Mante had scrambled aboard the *Hanley* to be reunited with his beloved dog. Mante then described to Kildall what had happened, and, as he told his tale, the astonishing truth of Hector's behavior dawned on them both. The *Simaloer* had set sail from Vancouver while Hector had been ashore, and to Mante's dismay and horror he was separated from his pet. It seemed Hector had been undaunted by this setback, and calmly inspected each ship in harbor until he found one he thought would reunite him with his master. Somehow he had picked the right vessel. Master and animal were never separated again, but the mystery of just how Hector came to choose the right ship remains unsolved.

chapter two
INVISIBLE BONDS

WE spend much of our lives close to our pets, but we may not always be aware of that secret bond that we share with them. Often, animals are aware of far more than we realize: they can guess our movements, know when we are coming home, or even be aware when tragedy has befallen us. We should never take our friendship with an animal for granted. Our pets value our love more than we can ever know.

In life, Chubby had been a good and loyal friend to his master, so after Jim Wicks died, the dog knew his time on earth was ended too, and gently pined away in his grief.

CHUBBY,
who died of a broken heart

T O THE WICKS FAMILY, Chubby was more than just a pet. The black, brown, and white dog was a true member of the family, and as events were to show, he shared their bad times as well as the good ones.

Chubby lived with Jim and Mary Wicks in their house in the town of Armadale, south of Perth in Western Australia. He was part kelpie—a breed of sheepdog—and had a kind, friendly appearance. He belonged to both Jim and Mary Wicks, but it was with Jim that Chubby shared a special bond. So it was no surprise when this good-natured dog became an important companion to Jim Wicks when disaster hit the family in 1991. A fire swept through and destroyed their home, and Jim was very badly burned. During the many months of illness that followed, Chubby stayed close to Jim, as if guarding and protecting him from any further harm. When the house was rebuilt and Jim was able to sit outside on the veranda, he would throw a ball for Chubby to fetch and the two spent many hours in each other's company. Chubby, who himself was no youngster, seemed to help and relax Jim through his slow and painful recovery. When Jim and Mary had gone to sleep, Chubby fulfilled another important role as a guard dog. His part-kelpie breeding made him an alert, fierce, and reassuring presence outside the house. The months passed and Jim recovered from his burns, but by May 1993, he had fallen ill again.

A DOG'S INTUITION

The doctors were concerned about Jim's condition; he had suffered from bad headaches for a while and was very ill. They were not the only ones to express concern. One night in May 1993, Jim heard Chubby barking at the back door. When Jim opened the door, Chubby ran into the house, headed straight for the bedroom and sat down by Jim's side of the bed. Jim and Mary both knew this was unusual behavior, since Chubby was very much an outdoor dog who was not allowed to enter the house, and he had never before shown any desire to do so. Yet, here he was by Jim's bedside, refusing to be moved.

The next day Chubby still refused to leave the house and instead stayed close to Jim. Neither Jim nor Mary could explain Chubby's behavior, but they let him stay inside with his master. The next day Jim suffered a stroke and fell into a coma; he died soon afterward in the hospital.

Back at home, it was obvious that Chubby knew exactly what had occurred. Indeed, it seemed clear that the animal had sensed what was going to happen to Jim. Chubby now sat listlessly on the veranda not eating and scarcely drinking. Then, a week after Jim had died, Chubby too passed away peacefully. Although there was no obvious reason for his death, Mary Wicks was certain she knew what had happened to old Chubby. Separated from his beloved master, she believed the faithful dog had simply died of a broken heart.

The THRUSH'S *final song*

THE CLOSE AND INVISIBLE LINKS THAT EXIST between pets and their owners can develop slowly over the years, and can exist even with animals that have been discovered in the wild. This was the case with William Milburn and a beautiful little song thrush whose pet name, sadly, has not survived the telling of the story.

William Milburn lived in Jarrow-on-Tyne in the northeast of England. He was well known locally as a bird lover who cared for many wild birds that had been ill or injured, or for young birds whose parents had been killed. He also cared for eggs that had been abandoned, keeping them warm while they hatched, and then played mother and father to the little hatchlings until they were old enough to fend for themselves. William was very knowledgeable about birds and their behavior and character, and appeared to understand them. Certainly, the many birds he looked after over the years seemed to be fond of their kindhearted master. Most of the time William encouraged his feathered friends to be independent, so that once they had grown to adulthood or recovered from the injuries, they

William Milburn had been a good friend to the pet thrush, so when the man passed away the little bird sang a final tribute to her companion.

could fly away again. As much as William loved birds in his house and garden, he understood that their true beauty was in the wild. And so, as he got older and the birds flew away, there were fewer and fewer of his pets around the home. Eventually, in the 1950s, there was just one bird left—a song thrush. Song thrushes, as their name suggests, have a beautiful repertoire of melodies, which, on a quiet evening, can be heard a half mile away. William had raised this particular thrush as a fledgling and he was very attached to her. She was also a particularly beautiful singer. Nonetheless, he encouraged her independence and did not keep her in a cage.

A BEAUTIFUL SONG

Indeed, the bird was free to fly around the house, yard, and garden. Yet, whereas all his other birds eventually flew away, this one thrush did not. Instead, the bird chose to stay with William, sometimes perching on his shoulder or even on his head as he walked around. Visitors marveled at how, whenever William appeared in the room, the little bird would burst out into the most beautiful song.

The female thrush was good company for William as he grew older. Yet time was taking its toll, and a bad bout of the flu confined the elderly man to bed. As William lay ill, the thrush kept him company, but was very quiet, barely singing at all.

Within a few days, William was dead. The thrush stayed in the house while the old man's body was laid out in his coffin for three days. During all this time, no one heard a single sound out of the bird. The funeral day dawned and still the thrush, which was roaming freely in the house, stayed absolutely silent. Then, as the pallbearers began to lift the coffin and move it slowly out of the house toward the hearse, the thrush dramatically burst into song, as if singing a last farewell to her departed owner. The beautiful, sorrowful singing continued until the hearse was out of sight, and the thrush fell silent once more. It never sang again. The next morning relatives came back to the house and found that the little bird, like its master, had died.

THE MAJORITY OF STORIES of psychic bonds between humans and the animal kingdom involve familiar pets. Most of them are about dogs and cats, or possibly birds, and sometimes a horse or a rabbit. Such animals are cuddly and it is not difficult to see how special relationships can develop. However, strange as it might appear, there are also well-documented stories of strange, inexplicable bonds between humans—and bees. Traditions involving bees and humans stretch back far into the distant past. In the old English tradition of "Telling the bees" it was regarded as essential for a member of the family to inform the bees when their keeper had died. Usually this was undertaken by one of the younger members of the family, either by speaking the words out loud, or by tying a piece of black funeral crêpe to the hives.

On some occasions, however, events have gone further: sometimes the bees have held their own form of mourning for their dead keeper. One such occasion concerned John Zepka, a beekeeper from Adams, Massachusetts, who died in 1956. As the funeral party reached the grave for his interment, they noticed a swarm of bees. The swarm stayed motionless during the service, and then flew off. In February 1959, Ruby Parker noticed

THE BEES
who paid their last respects

how a swarm of bees attended the funeral of her beekeeping father, Charles D. Hitt, from Scott County, Missouri, even though it was a cold winter's day. The older bees never returned to the hive.

Bees can form deep bonds with the people who tend them. When beekeeper Sam Rogers died, his former charges joined startled mourners to say farewell at his graveside.

A RESPECTED KEEPER

One of the more remarkable stories concerns an old English beekeeper by the name of Sam Rogers. Sam was a postman and cobbler in a village in the county of Shropshire in England. Sam was also a well-known and much-respected beekeeper, who lavished great time and affection on the bees in his charge. Like most experienced keepers, he seemed to have an instinctive way of handling them. When Sam died in 1961, his children followed the old ways and went to each of their father's 14 hives, telling the bees inside of their keeper's death. This however was not the end of the bees' involvement in the story. Later, as family and friends gathered around Sam's grave a mile away, they were greeted by an extraordinary sight: thousands of bees from Sam's hives had flown from the hives and were now buzzing around the graveyard. Ignoring the many flowering trees nearby, the honeybees settled on the flowers and floral tributes that covered old Sam's coffin. There they stayed for half an hour, before leaving and returning to the hives. Those who witnessed it were deeply affected by the spectacle. Reverend John Ayling, the vicar who performed the ceremony that day, said he ought to try to find a rational explanation for the behavior of the insects. He added, "But if I didn't, I would say that those bees came to say good-bye to Sam."

FELIX WAS A DEVOTED FAMILY PET. The black-and-white tomcat lived with Robert King, his wife, and their young daughter in the St. Kilda district of east Melbourne, Australia. The cat loved them all, but was devoted to old Mr. King, Robert's father, with whom he had lived for many years. The pair were virtually inseparable. For the old man, Felix was a wonderful companion after the death of his wife; for the cat, his owner was a loving and dependable master.

The sad day finally arrived that old Mr. King died following a serious illness. Naturally the whole family mourned this loss, though their grief was tempered by the knowledge that the old gentleman had lived a long and happy life, and had been ill for some time. For Felix the cat, however, the death of his master was all-consuming. The pet, who had always been a quiet and calm sort of animal, was visibly distraught. He refused to eat the meals he normally gobbled down with glee; he wandered aimlessly around the house; he mewed, and he cried. Felix, it appeared, was inconsolable. The family was upset by their pet's obvious distress as they struggled to come to terms with their own sadness. After some days, in an attempt to soothe Felix's anguish, the family decided to take him for a ride in their car around Melbourne. Perhaps this would be something different for Felix to concentrate on, a new experience that would help to snap him out of his distress.

As far as Felix was concerned, the most important figure in his life was old Mr. King. When the elderly man died, the fluffy black-and-white tomcat felt it was only natural to seek out his grave.

FELIX
the faithful feline

All went well at first as the family and Felix drove through and around the city on a glorious sunny day. Then the car stopped at a traffic light, and something strange happened. Felix, who had been sitting quietly, clearly bemused by this new experience, suddenly became very alert. His fur bristled, his tail twitched, and he got to his feet in an obviously anxious state. Before the car had time to pull away from the traffic light, Felix abruptly leapt through one of the side windows, left open because of the warm day. Alarmed, the family members tried to call him back, and even tried to follow him, but it was no use. The traffic was heavy and Felix was seen disappearing into the distance. Soon he had vanished altogether.

A LONG WAIT

Coming so soon after the death of old Mr. King, Felix's abrupt departure was a cruel blow for the King family. Though they waited for him to return home to the house he knew and had loved, deep down they never expected to see Felix again.

It was with a doubly heavy heart that Mrs. King and her young daughter set off a week later to visit Mr. King's grave and lay some flowers at his graveside. When they reached the cemetery, however, they were greeted by an unexpected sight. There, pacing determinedly up and down by the graveside, was none other than Felix the cat.

With his distinctive scar and slightly crooked tail, Felix was larger than life and clearly delighted to see Mrs. King and her daughter. Mrs. King was baffled. How on earth had Felix found the cemetery, never mind the grave? It was more than five miles from the spot at which Felix had jumped from the car, and the animal had never been there before in his life.

Now, however, Felix could not be separated from the place. Several times Mrs. King and her daughter tried to take Felix from old Mr. King's grave, but each time the cat leapt out of the car before they had even reached the cemetery gate, and returned to his vigil. There was no escaping it. Felix was determined to stay "on guard" for his master even at his grave. Eventually, the King family arranged for the cemetery staff to feed the animal, whom they visited regularly, but they were never able to persuade him to leave. Until his dying day, Felix remained faithful to his late master and stayed loyally by his graveside.

K ING WAS A WELL-NAMED PET. Dark, strong, and imposing, the
German Shepherd dog undoubtedly had a regal air about him.
But King also recognized a higher authority: his master Philip
Friedman, to whom he was devoted.

Philip and Clara Friedman ran a grocery store in Brooklyn, New
York, in the 1930s. By 1934 Philip, now an elderly man, was ill, and his
family somehow knew he was dying. Certainly King seemed to know.
From his vantage point out in the store's backyard, the animal sensed what

The close bond between
King and his master meant
that the German Shepherd
knew where, and when, his
master had been buried.

KING, the DOG
who knew where his
master was buried

was happening to his owner and best friend, and was deeply
upset. It was not just his mournful look that revealed King's
inner dread, but his whimpers and cries as he sat under the
dying man's window. As old Philip began to slip away, King
became more and more anguished. When the proud old man
eventually died in November, it was evident that King knew
what had happened to the master to whom he had been
devoted. The dog reached up with his paws and scratched on
the window, as if to say good-bye to Philip for the last time,
and then let out a deep and sorrowful howl.

King was kept shut safely in the yard while the family went about the sad business of laying out the body and arranging the funeral, which ran smoothly and with dignity. Philip's pet, meanwhile, kept up clear signs of grief at his master's passing. As the family mourned at home, King kept quiet during prayers, but at other times howled from his yard and from inside the kennel his master had built for him. No one knew how to comfort the animal in his distress.

Then, three days later, King escaped. A strong gust of wind blew the yard door open, and before anyone could close it, the hound had vanished. The distraught family and neighbors began to search for King, upset at the thought that the dead man's grieving dog was out in the city all alone with his sorrow. The hunt, however, was in vain. Even a small ad placed in the local newspaper produced no sightings of King. It appeared he had disappeared for good.

Then one day a member of the family had an idea. Why not visit the cemetery where Philip was buried, in case King had turned up there? The idea was at first ridiculed—King had been safely shut up for the interment and had never even been to the cemetery—but no one had any better idea, and so off they went.

There, at the Mount Hebron Cemetery in Brooklyn, the family was surprised to see a dog's footprints in the snow close to Philip's grave. Intrigued, they asked an attendant if he had noticed a large German Shepherd at the cemetery. To their amazement, he confirmed he had, and not only that, it seemed this dog turned up at the grave every day, lay down across it, and cried and whined in clear distress. If anyone tried to come close, the dog would growl in warning. What is more, said the cemetery attendant, the dog turned up regularly each day at 2 P.M. The Friedman family looked at each other in amazement. Philip's burial had taken place at exactly 2 P.M.

The next day a member of the family waited by the grave to see if King would arrive. Shortly after 2 P.M. the animal duly appeared in the distance. The family member called out his name in an attempt to get the grieving animal to come home with him. Instead, King stared briefly ahead for a moment, then turned around and vanished. No one saw him again. King had gone to be reunited with his master.

O FTEN A CLOSE BOND DEVELOPS between a human and an animal when that person has performed some kindness to the animal. In many cases the creature seeks to repay its debt of gratitude. Such was the case with the story of Hugh Perkins and the unexpected friend he made in the 1950s. Hugh, who was then age 12, lived a quiet life in West Virginia, and often used to play happily on his own out in the backyard. One day a pigeon flew into the yard. Hugh was intrigued by the gray bird; it had an aluminum band on one of its legs and so it was clearly some kind of homing or racing pigeon. Despite this, however, the pigeon certainly was in no hurry to return to wherever it had come

The comforting
PIGEON

from. Hugh began feeding his new, feathered friend and the pigeon gradually seemed more and more at ease and at home. The youngster would talk to the bird, and it seemed to respond to the kindly tone of his voice. There was no way of telling whether the bird had been lost or hungry, or just needed a friend, but it quickly became more comfortable in Hugh's presence. Indeed, within a few days the pigeon had firmly established itself as Hugh's pet and the two became good friends. The youngster even discovered that the band on the bird's leg had an identification number on it—167.

A young boy helped out a pigeon that had fluttered into the backyard; so when the boy later became sick himself the bird repaid the kindness by flying 100 miles to be at his young friend's hospital bedside.

A DANGEROUS ILLNESS

The friendship continued throughout the following year, with Hugh regularly feeding and talking to his pet. One day, however, the youngster fell suddenly and seriously ill. His parents, desperately worried for Hugh's health, drove him 100 miles across the mountains, to get him to a large hospital where he could receive care. At the medical center, the doctors quickly operated on Hugh and he was pronounced to be out of danger. However, he was still very weak from his ordeal and was told he had to spend time in a hospital bed while his strength returned to him.

The night after the operation there was a snowstorm and, as he lay awake in bed, Hugh could hear a gentle tapping on the window. At first he assumed it was the effects of the storm blowing branches against the windowpane. But the tapping persisted and the noise was more regular and orderly than a swaying tree might make. Hugh looked carefully, and there it was: a pigeon was huddled up against the cold and snow, tapping his beak on the windowpane. Hugh was too weak to get out of bed, so he called to a nurse to open the window. Sure enough, as soon as she did, the half-frozen bird hopped inside. Hugh knew right away who this bird was, and the aluminum band on the bird's leg confirmed it: the number was 167. It was Hugh's pet homing pigeon. Hugh had shown this bird great kindness, feeding it and offering it unconditional friendship. Now the same bird had flown 100 miles through a snowstorm to return the favor to its friend in his hour of need.

THE BOND THAT DEVELOPS BETWEEN AN INDIVIDUAL and his or her pet may not only last for a lifetime, but can endure beyond. For some pets, loyalty to a person is not only confined to this world. This at least explains the extraordinary story of Shep, the sheepdog, and his devotion to one man.

The black-and-white sheepdog lived for many years with Francis McMahon at his home in Illinois. The pair were practically inseparable, whether they were going on walks together or sitting quietly at home listening to the radio. This contented life went on for many years, with the loyal Shep always protective of his master's well-being and safety. Francis, too, trusted in his quiet, undemonstrative dog. However, one day he failed to take notice of his dog's warning behavior, with disastrous consequences.

It happened when Francis was going to descend his basement stairs to do some repair work. Shep started barking furiously. This was very unlike the sheepdog's normal behavior, so Francis looked around. Seeing nothing out of the ordinary, he continued down the stairs. After a few seconds, however, he lost his footing on one of the stairs and fell headlong into the basement. It was an accident Shep had apparently foreseen and feared.

SHEP'S *long wait*

HIS MASTER'S COMMAND

An ambulance was called, and the unfortunate Francis was rushed immediately to the hospital, with Shep following in a relative's car. It soon became apparent that Francis had fractured his skull in the accident and was seriously ill. However, he was conscious, and indeed, as he was being wheeled out of the emergency room Francis was able to call out to

The bond that existed between sheepdog Shep and his owner was so strong that even when his master passed away, the dog refused to leave the spot where he had last seen him alive.

Shep, who was sitting in an agitated state in a corridor by the front of the hospital. Francis told the animal that he would be okay, and also told Shep to wait for him at the front of the hospital. Obedient and loyal as ever, Shep did as Francis asked and waited by the front steps of the hospital for his master to return. Unfortunately, Francis' condition worsened, and within just a few hours of talking to Shep, he died. Shep was on the other side of the hospital when this happened, and remained in his position as he had been told to do. But as they wheeled the body of Francis through a rear door of the hospital, the dog let out an anguished, sorrowful howl. He did not need to see Francis' body to know that he had passed away. Yet despite Francis' death, Shep stayed where he was, near to the steps of the front of the hospital. From then on, this area became the dog's new home. Shep kept a lonely vigil for his departed master, a vigil that lasted a full 12 years. Although, deep down, Shep knew his master was gone, he felt that by obeying Francis' final order to him he could somehow remain close to the man he loved. Until, that is, it was time for Shep himself to join his master in a better place.

B OB HAD NOT BEEN WITH THE FAMILY FOR VERY LONG, and was barely more than a puppy, but the black-and-white collie was devoted to his master Roy, a young Englishman and army officer. When they were at home, the pair were inseparable, and Roy and his wife both marveled at Bob's playful nature and seemingly boundless energy. The year, however, was 1915, and like many young men of his generation, Roy was called up to fight for his country in what was to become known as World War I. Roy's wife knew she would be anxious when Roy bade her farewell and set off to France to fight against the Germans, but she was

Though his master was miles away on a battlefield, Bob the collie suddenly sensed when the army officer's life was in danger and howled at the exact moment of his death.

BOB the DOG'S
vision of the trenches

unprepared for the change in Bob. During the months after Roy left, Bob became quiet and withdrawn. Gone was the playfulness she and Roy had seen before. The young dog was, she noted, "almost morose" in his behavior.

Bob got into the habit of sleeping in his mistress' bedroom. Each night the collie would settle down just inside the door, and each morning he would awaken her by trotting over and licking her hand to say "good morning." It was almost as if by keeping close to his master's wife, he was staying close to his master himself.

This arrangement continued, with Bob showing no signs of regaining his high spirits, until the morning of September 15, 1915. On that day Roy's wife woke as usual, but was surprised to find that she had not been awakened by the routine greeting from Bob. In fact, Bob was nowhere to be seen. She called twice, and eventually, slowly, the young collie crept out from underneath the bed. He gave the woman's hand a brief lick, then immediately crept back underneath again.

This was not Bob's only unusual behavior. Normally he would go out in the morning for a walk, but that day he would have none of it. His nose was dry, he was running a temperature, and in general he was behaving strangely. Concerned at the dog's listless state, Roy's wife decided to take him by car to the veterinarian. Usually, the collie leapt at the chance of a trip in the car, but on this occasion she practically had to carry him to the vehicle. Despite her concerns, the doctor assured Roy's wife there was nothing obviously wrong with the animal, and the pair went home. But, still Bob behaved oddly. He refused his food and lay glumly on the floor, looking up at his mistress with big, sad eyes. She thought that it seemed almost as if Bob was trying to tell her something.

Just as Roy's wife was contemplating a second visit to the veterinarian, the dog suddenly let out a terrible, haunting howl. For several minutes Bob was inconsolable, and even when he had stopped howling, he continued to moan and whine in a way that was totally out of character. Then, gradually his temperature went down, and though he refused food for several days, Bob seemed to recover.

Roy's wife was bemused until four days later when she received the news that Roy had been killed in action. She learned from another officer that her brave husband had been shot dead as he rose from the trenches to go "over the top" against the enemy.

She also learned the date and time he had died: the precise moment that Bob had begun his sad and mournful howling. The pet's behavior on September 15 now made sense. Bob had somehow known that his master's life was in terrible danger that day. The poor animal had been aware of his master's grim fate the moment it occurred, and had howled uncontrollably, at the terrible loss that both his mistress and he now shared.

The selfless devotion of Greyfriars' Bobby is one of the most moving stories of friendship between a man and his dog. The terrier guarded his master's grave for 14 years.

JUST OCCASIONALLY, AN ACT OF DEVOTION AND LOYALTY is so overwhelming that it can live on in a society's memory to inspire later generations. This was the case with the remarkable story of Greyfriars' Bobby from the nineteenth century. Bobby was a young, brave Skye terrier who belonged to a policeman named John Gray. Gray—or Auld Jock as he was known—worked as a policeman in Edinburgh, Scotland. The life of a police officer was a difficult and dangerous one, and for two years Bobby was the perfect companion for Auld Jock as he patrolled the streets of the city late at night. The work took its toll, however, and one day in 1858, John fell ill. Within a short time he died, much to the distress of the young terrier. Bobby was among the mourners at his master's funeral, which concluded with a graveside ceremony at the Greyfriars Kirkyard (graveyard) in Edinburgh where John was buried. Afterward, relatives took the distraught Bobby home, where they discussed what would become of him. But Bobby was in no mood to be separated from his master. That night he slipped free and made his way back to the graveyard.

GREYFRIARS' BOBBY,
the devoted terrier

A LOYAL DOG

Although the gates were usually locked, Bobby managed to get inside, probably when patrolling police officers unlocked the yard. After all, Bobby knew all about the routines of the police from his late master. In the morning, the curator of the burial ground, James Brown, found Bobby lying on John Gray's grave. Now, it was against the rules to allow dogs into the graveyard, so James Brown made the little terrier leave the yard. The next morning, however, Bobby was there again, and once more James Brown had to usher him out. On the third morning, when Bobby had returned yet again to his master's grave, the graveyard curator took pity on the little animal. The weather was wet and cold and the curator gave the dog some food, and from then on Bobby was a permanent feature in the graveyard. Sometimes, in very bad weather, Bobby was given shelter in a nearby house. But he was never happy away from the graveyard and made his unhappiness obvious. Bobby's incredible vigil lasted until 1872 and his own death—a remarkable 14 years after his master had passed away. Fittingly, the terrier's body was buried close to the grave of John Gray. By now the little dog's example had become an inspiration for the people of Edinburgh and many people living further away. A statue was put up to commemorate Bobby's devotion to his master and visitors still visit the graveyard to see the monument. There are regular enactments of Bobby's story and a movie has been made of the tale. Far more powerful than any statue or movie, however, is the simple example of Bobby's selfless and loyal behavior, an enduring tribute to that incredible bond that exists between human and animal.

FLORa
& maia's
welcoming instinct

THE TWO SIAMESE CATS, FLORA AND MAIA, lived with Judith and Geoffrey Preston-Jones in the beautiful countryside of Kent in southern England. They had a special bond with Judith; she recalls that they were "very much my cats." In common with their breed, they were both handsome and highly intelligent, but Maia and Flora also shared one other special quality: they always seemed to know just when their mistress was due to arrive home. It did not seem to matter which hour of the day or evening, the two Siamese had the uncanny knack of being able to anticipate Judith's homecoming, even when she had been traveling from some distance away. As soon as the pair knew that Judith was about to come home, they would start to show telltale signs of anticipation and excitement. If the weather was fine and warm, especially in summer, then Flora and Maia would rush out into the front garden to sit there until Judith returned. However, if the weather was cold or wet, they would stay inside in the dry and warm. Yet, still they would show they knew Judith's arrival was imminent by waiting by the door.

STRANGE ABILITIES

So noteworthy were the cats' antics that for one period in the 1990s, Geoffrey and Judith each kept a diary of the pets and their reactions. These diaries show that when Judith was away from the house for longer periods or when she returned from work in the evenings, the two animals usually would start to show excitement about 10 minutes before her arrival. As Judith said, "They would be asleep like zombies, then they would suddenly wake up when I was coming home. My husband always knew when I was coming home. I think it's an ability all animals have. I cannot really account for it."

There were a few exceptions to this behavior, however. On one occasion when the weather was very cold, the cats gave up their normal waiting position and, following the traditional feline urge to keep warm, they stayed snugly by the warm boiler. On another occasion, Flora and Maia failed to anticipate Judith's arrival home. This was apparently because a man had come to fix the broken washing machine, and the shy cats had fled upstairs to hide from the stranger.

The most remarkable occurrence came one evening when Judith returned at around 9:40 P.M. She had been at a meeting in a village some three miles away. Geoffrey informed her that on this occasion the cats' welcoming instinct had gone very wrong. He reported that the pair had gotten into their usual restless state at 9 P.M., and so accordingly Geoffrey had expected his wife home by around 9:10 P.M. But she had not arrived, suggesting the cats' early warning system was not infallible after all. Geoffrey was not prepared, however, for Judith's subsequent explanation of events. She had in fact left the meeting earlier and got in her car ready to drive home, but then remembered she had to speak to a friend about some matter and had gone back to the meeting place until 9:30 P.M. Flora and Maia had reacted just as Judith had first gotten into the car, which was at precisely 9 P.M.

No matter what time of day or night she was returning, or how far she had traveled, the beautiful Siamese cats Flora and Maia always knew exactly when their beloved mistress was about to arrive.

SOME PETS SHOW THEIR PSYCHIC LINKS with humans not only by knowing when a person is coming home, but also by knowing if that person is calling home on the telephone. There are a number of well-documented stories of animals that seem to know who is on the other end of the line when the phone rings. For example, David Waite from Oxfordshire, England, reports that while he is away on business and his parents are house-sitting, his cat Godzilla will respond to the phone ringing only if it is David calling home; other calls Godzilla ignores. Meanwhile a gray parrot, called Kerry, from North Yorkshire, England, shouts out, "Michelle" or "Jeanine" when the telephone rings, according to which of the two sisters is calling home. But one of the most remarkable stories of pets who anticipate their masters comes from the Zaugg family in Switzerland. Meo was, to the casual glance, an everyday kind of black-and-white cat. During the 1970s, he lived quietly with the family at their home in the tranquil, small town of Biel, not far from Bern. However, Meo was certainly no ordinary cat, and he displayed an extraordinary talent, an ability described by family member, Helena Zaugg. Helena said Meo, whom she had found abandoned in a street in Bern,

Hans Zaugg's family knew when he was on the way home, as his devoted cat Meo would always react the same way.

meo,
the telepathic cat

was particularly close to her father Hans, with whom the cat seemed to share a special relationship. After Mr.

Zaugg had retired from regular work as an electrical engineer, he sometimes used to work for someone he knew in Aargau, a short train ride away. While Mr. Zaugg was away from home, he would call home sometimes to check that everyone was okay, and to reassure his family that all was well with him.

PSYCHIC AWARENESS

According to Helena, however, the family always knew when he was about to call. One minute before the telephone began to ring, Meo would become agitated and flop down right next to the telephone, almost as if he wanted to answer it himself. This was particularly unusual because the good-natured Meo never behaved in this way with any other phone calls. But this was not the limit of Meo's psychic awareness. Mr. Zaugg used to come home by train to the station at Biel, then rode the rest of the way home on a scooter. The family knew precisely when their father's train had come in, because Meo would move next to the front door 20 minutes before Mr. Zaugg came through it. Twenty minutes was the length of time for the scooter ride. Sometimes, though, Mr. Zaugg would arrive a little earlier than expected on a different train, and he would phone from the station to tell his family he was back early. This, too, the family would know in advance, because on such occasions Meo would once more sit by the phone moments before it rang. Then, realizing what the phone call meant, he would pad his way over to the front door to await his master's return. It seemed that Meo did not only know when his master would call, but also why he was calling. Truly, Meo was no ordinary cat.

a SMALL, SPANIEL-SIZE, MIXED-BREED DOG, Rusty was the kind of dog you could not easily ignore. Before he shared a home with sisters Elizabeth and Sue Bryan, he had spent some time living on the streets and he was a lively and tough character. As Sue said: "Rusty was a streetwise dog, like Tramp from the Disney film *Lady and the Tramp*. He was extremely intuitive."

Certainly Rusty lived up to his reputation for being intuitive. The house that Sue and Elizabeth shared was in Crawley, a small town in the beautiful county of Sussex, England, and close to the major airport of Gatwick. The location was well suited for Elizabeth's work, since she was a flight attendant on a major British airline. Although this job can have its glamorous side involving travel to far-off locations, the work of a flight attendant is also very demanding and occasionally grueling. Some of the hardest aspects of the job are the unpredictability of the hours, the long shifts, and the irregular patterns of work it

Rusty's
airplane insight

When Sue Bryan wanted to know when her flight attendant sister Elizabeth was due home, she simply watched the reaction of Rusty, their insightful dog.

can bring. This means that it is sometimes hard
for those left at home to know when their loved
one will return. In the Bryan household,
however, this was not a problem, as Sue Bryan
knew exactly when her sister's plane was
touching down at the airport: she only had to
look at Rusty's reaction.

A SPECIAL ATTACHMENT
Although Rusty got along well enough with
Sue, he had formed a special attachment to
Elizabeth and was devoted to his mistress. As a
result he kept a very close eye on her departures
and homecomings. The instant that Elizabeth's
plane landed, Rusty would prick up his ears,
leap onto the sofa, and then stare intently out
the window while he waited for her to arrive
home. It did not matter whether her plane was
late, or what irregular shift pattern she was
working. Indeed, Elizabeth worked on long- and
short-haul flights, as well as day flights and night

flights. Nor did it matter that Gatwick is one of
the busiest airports in the world, with planes
constantly landing and taking off; Rusty always
knew the moment that her flight touched
down. The dog was so reliable that sister Sue
would use his behavior as if it were some kind
of airline timetable. No matter how far Elizabeth
had flown, or how unexpected her flight was,
for the three years that he shared their house,
Rusty never made a mistake. Once the plane
had landed, Rusty would calm down again. But
then as soon as Elizabeth's car reached the
traffic circle near their home, he would get
excited again.

Sue never failed to be amazed at Rusty's
ability. "He could never have known when
Elizabeth was coming home, either the day or
the time of day. But I always knew when her
plane had landed because he reacted the same
way every time. It was extraordinary."

chapter three

SAVING LIVES

PETS can provide us with many things. They give us love, friendship, and companionship. They make us laugh, and sometimes cry. Yet, there are times when the relationship is even more important than that. There are times when pets can save our lives. Animals are tuned in to the world around them, and they can sense what is happening before we are aware of it. Sometimes they can even predict what is going to happen. They also know when we are in danger, and do their best to help, sometimes with startling results.

CUDDLES,
the life-saving cat

I**T WAS A VERY SPECIAL EVENING** for Dede Summerscales.
The next day was going to be the happiest of her life—her
wedding day—and she had spent her remaining hours as a
single woman ensuring that all the preparations were in place.
Finally, after the exertion of a very exhilarating but tiring day, she
was looking forward to a good night's sleep.

So it was that on the evening of September 8, 1978, Dede
finally finished her work and snuggled into bed at her house in
Kalamunda, Western Australia. The early spring weather was cool, so
she switched on her electric blanket. As she sank into the blankets
she felt comfortable and warm. Just then she heard a noise at the
door. Puzzled, she went to find out what was causing it, and to her
surprise saw her pet cat, Cuddles, standing there. The cat jumped
into the room and then sprang up onto Dede's bed, clearly intent
on staying there for the night. Dede was surprised at this behavior,
since the cat always slept downstairs and never with her. Still,
perhaps she was excited about the wedding and wanted to spend
this final night with her mistress. Dede, however, was too tired to
think much about it, and soon fell into a deep and untroubled sleep.

A SPECIAL PRESENT

Within a few hours Dede was abruptly awakened from her slumber. As she awoke she found Cuddles sitting next to her face, licking her, and making an unusual crying noise. A little annoyed at being woken, and wondering why her cat was acting so oddly, Dede sat upright. It was then that she noticed the strong smell of smoke in the room. Looking down quickly, she could see exactly what was causing the smoke: her electric blanket was melting and catching fire. Dede leapt out of bed and swiftly unplugged the blanket and stamped out the fire, angry that she had left the blanket on while she slept, but relieved that she had awoken when she had. Still shaken by the events, Dede eventually got back to sleep.

Dede's father examined the blanket early the next day and found that a connection had come loose and that the blanket had begun smoldering. It was now clear that if she had not awakened when she did, Dede might have been badly burned or killed by the fire. By now, of course, Dede realized why Cuddles had come into her room late in the evening and awakened her in the middle of the night. Cuddles had been aware of the danger and had acted to save her mistress.

From that happy day onward, Dede knew that Cuddles was more than just a family pet. She was indeed a true and faithful friend who had given her mistress the best of wedding presents: life itself.

Bride-to-be Dede shall never forget the devotion of her pet cat, Cuddles. The resourceful animal saved her life from a fire on the eve of the young woman's wedding.

aCTS OF BRAVERY AND COURAGE come in all shapes and sizes. So, too, do heroes. One animal hero who proved that you do not need to be physically large or strong to be a savior, was Bib, a yellow canary. Bib belonged to an elderly woman known locally as Aunt Tess. Together, they lived in Hermitage, Tennessee, where Bib made a cheerful companion for the old lady. His constant singing and chirpy character brought comfort to Aunt Tess in the twilight of her life.

However, because of her age, Aunt Tess was vulnerable living in her house alone with only her pet canary for company. Although she chose to live that

BIB'S
brave sacrifice

way, her niece, who lived nearby, kept a close eye on the elderly lady. Each night the niece would check to see if the lights were on in Aunt Tess' house to indicate that everything was all right. It was an informal system, but it worked well enough.

He may have been only small, but Bib the brave canary had the courage and the strength to save Aunt Tess' life.

One rainy, windswept evening the niece made her usual check on Tess' lights, and saw through the stormy night air that the lights were on. Reassured that all was well with her aunt, the young woman drew her own curtains and settled down with her husband for a quiet night in, safely sheltered from the harsh elements.

JUST IN TIME

Halfway through the evening, however, the couple heard a loud tap-tapping at the windowpane. Taking it at first for a branch blowing against the house, the pair ignored it. But the tapping continued, and it was persistent, almost urgent, in nature. Now concerned, the niece hurried over to the curtains, drew them apart, and saw a small yellow bird on the outside of the window. The poor creature was drenched and battered by the weather. It was Bib. Taken aback at the sight of the canary, the niece sensed that something might be wrong at Aunt Tess' home. She and her husband raced over to the house as quickly as they could, but they received no answer to their urgent knocking. When they let themselves in they saw why: Aunt Tess was lying on the floor in the hallway. Next to her was a pool of blood, and signs that she may have hit her head on a table as she stumbled and fell. Fortunately, they were just in time, and were able to have her taken to the hospital for urgent medical treatment.

Tess made a good recovery and was able to return home. For Bib, however, the news was not so good. The exertion of tapping on the niece's window had been too much, and the canary had collapsed and died on the spot. They found its little body by the window at which it had been tapping. Tess and her family were deeply saddened by his death. But they knew it wasn't in vain. If Bib had not bravely sounded the alarm the only way he could, Aunt Tess would have passed away. A loyal pet, Bib had made the ultimate sacrifice—to save the life of his mistress and friend.

DOLPHINS ARE AMONG THE MOST intelligent of mammals, and these enchanting animals certainly seem to enjoy the company of humans. At times, however, the relationship has extended beyond mere playfulness and has involved life-and-death situations. On one occasion in 1967, for example, a group of dolphins in the Black Sea made it clear to the crew of a fishing boat that they required human help. Surrounding the vessel and pointing it in a certain direction, they guided the boat to a buoy, in whose rope a baby dolphin had become trapped. The fishing crew was able to free the creature quickly, and the dolphins showed their delight and gratitude by escorting the boat all the way back to harbor. Somehow the dolphins had known the fishermen would be able to help them.

No human ever had a better friend than Beaky, the exuberant and intrepid dolphin, who saved diver Keith Monery's life.

BEAKY
the dolphin saves a diver

The most startling story, though, is that of Beaky, a bottle-nosed dolphin who lived off the rugged Cornish coast in England in the 1970s. Although a wild animal, Beaky became a familiar and popular sight with schoolchildren and divers in the area for a number of years. This remarkable 12-foot dolphin was credited

with saving no fewer than four human lives on separate occasions. One was that of a crew member of a cargo boat who fell overboard without a life jacket. The man certainly would have died had Beaky not kept him afloat until he was rescued. The most moving account, however, involved diver Keith Monery who was diving off Penzance in 1976.

DISTRESS SIGNAL

He was an experienced diver, but on this occasion Keith got into difficulties in rough seas. His life jacket had filled with water, and although he jettisoned his diving weights, he was having trouble staying afloat. Aware that his life was in danger, Keith used the diving distress signal—waving a clenched fist—to call urgently for help. A fellow diver, Hazel Carswell, saw the signal and, realizing Keith was in trouble, tried to help. But before she could even get close, another helper swam powerfully to the rescue: it was Beaky. The dolphin had appeared on the scene, apparently from nowhere, and was somehow aware of Keith's state of distress. As

the diver struggled to keep afloat, the dolphin quickly swam underneath him and, with his powerful nose, repeatedly nudged the stricken diver up to the surface. Time and time again, as Keith fell back under the surface, Beaky pushed him back up again. Without the animal's help, Keith may well have drowned in those choppy seas. Instead, Beaky kept the diver afloat until Hazel could swim over to help with the rescue. Even then, Beaky stayed nearby, making sure the pair of divers was able to stay on the surface until a rescue boat arrived to get Keith out of the water. Only then did Beaky swim off, aware that his life-saving help was no longer needed.

Saving Lives

LULU WAS AN UNUSUAL KIND OF PET. She was a Vietnamese pot-bellied pig. Jo-Ann and Jack Altsman, from Beaver Falls, Pennsylvania, originally had bought the pig as a present for their grown-up daughter Jackie. But Jackie had not been keen on having a pig around the house, and after "baby sitting" the animal over one weekend, Jo-Ann and Jack took Lulu back to their house with them. They became very fond of the pig, even as she ballooned in size from a few-pound piglet to a 150-pound adult, and decided to keep her. Soon afterward, they would be very glad they had.

One day in August 1998, Jo-Ann was at home when she collapsed with terrible pains in her chest. She knew it was a heart attack, having suffered one before. Lying helpless on the floor, she was in great pain and unable to reach the phone to call for help. She began to fear she would die alone—except that she was not alone. Sensing the woman's distress, Lulu waddled over to look at her. Great tears began to fall down her snout, and she made the most unusual sounds. Jo-Ann realized that the pig was crying for her. But Lulu had not just come over to show

LULU tHE PIG
stops the traffic

She may have been an unlikely heroine, but Lulu the pot-bellied Vietnamese pig knew just what to do to save Jo-Ann Altsman's life.

her sorrow. Aware that her mistress quickly needed help, the pig dashed as fast as she could toward the back door where the Altsmans had a dog flap. Although she was far too large for this modest hole, Lulu somehow squeezed her way through, cutting her skin in the process, and ran into the yard. There she managed to force open the yard gate and run into the street. Lulu had never left the house on her own before, and certainly never without a leash, so this taste of the outdoors must have been bewildering, but somehow she knew just what to do.

GETTING HELP

Each time a car approached on the street, Lulu ran out in front of it and lay down. She repeated this extraordinary behavior several times, with most motorists avoiding the bleeding pig and driving on past. Every now and again Lulu would rush back into the house—through the dog flap—to check Jo-Ann before rushing back into the road again. Eventually, after many attempts, Lulu managed to persuade one driver

to stop. Concerned for the animal's welfare, the motorist got out to investigate. This was when Lulu put the next part of her plan into action. As the man approached, Lulu sprang up and trotted into the house, making sure the puzzled driver followed her. As he approached the house, the man shouted through the door that the owner's pig was in distress. A startled Jo-Ann replied that *she* was the one in distress, and begged the man to dial 9-1-1. Help arrived and Jo-Ann was rushed to the hospital where doctors told her that she would have died had she been delayed another 15 minutes. As it was, she made a good recovery.

Meanwhile, Lulu, who was bruised and cut from the dog flap, had tried to join Jo-Ann in the ambulance, but the rescue team thought this might be pushing things a little too far. No matter, Lulu had already done her job. Sensing danger, she had undoubtedly saved her owner's life. The Altsmans were certainly glad they had kept this remarkable animal.

THE NORMAL DESIRE OF PETS, understandably, is to help the person or family whom they love. It is usually within the family that the invisible bond between humans and animals develops, fostering the desire of pets to come to the rescue of their owners. Yet, sometimes a special animal will help out a human even though they have never met before, and may never do so again. One such pet was Scotty.

Scotty was an amiable mixed-breed dog who lived with his family in the Ozark Mountain Region of Arkansas, near the beautiful Buffalo National River. The countryside around the river is one of the most attractive and unspoiled spots in that part of the United States, with many wild animals and a rugged landscape that is always popular with visitors. Although the area is quite safe, it is not the kind of place where you would want your child to be wandering around alone, at night and in winter. That, however, is

Saved by SCOTTY

what happened to one unfortunate family. They had taken advantage of the pale wintry sunshine to take a walk through part of the river area. However, Misty Hagar, who was a foster child, somehow became separated from the rest of the party late in the afternoon. Within a few minutes, she was lost in the wild terrain, and her family soon missed her and contacted a rescue team to search for her. The family and experts had good reason to worry. During the day's sunshine the weather had been deceptively warm, but now the temperature was plummeting. Even worse, the weather forecasters were predicting a snowstorm that night, and all Misty was wearing was a light jacket and an equally light pair of pants.

*When schoolgirl Misty got
lost in the wilderness her
family feared the worst.
However, Scotty the dog made
sure the young girl survived
the dangers of the forest.*

RACE AGAINST TIME

Knowing they were in a race against the elements, and that the
chances of Misty surviving the night on her own were slight, the
rescuers sprang into action. A helicopter with the latest infrared
thermal imaging equipment was brought in, while a hundred-strong
search party was boosted by the use of bloodhounds. However, as the
early evening turned into nightfall, there was still no sign of Misty.

Unknown to the search party, however, Misty was in safe hands, or
rather, paws. Scotty lived not far from the spot where Misty had
wandered. Out for a walk on his own, this white, mop-haired dog soon
sensed her presence and went to her aid. During that long, chilly night,
Scotty stayed right by Misty's side, allowing her to snuggle into his thick
coat for warmth. Even more remarkably, Scotty seemed to have hidden
the young girl's shoes to keep her from walking any more, which
prevented her from wandering aimlessly and possibly getting farther and
farther away from help. And so, when the deeply anxious search parties
found Misty by the river the next morning, she was safe and sound,
wrapped up in Scotty's warm fur. There were tears of joy and huge relief
at her discovery, but Scotty himself did not want any fuss. Knowing now
that his nighttime friend was safe, Scotty left Misty, her family, and rescuers
to their hugs, and quietly walked back home. His work had been done.

a CCIDENTS CAN SOMETIMES HAPPEN that make us feel that we have been foolish for not checking that we have been using equipment sensibly and carefully. Fortunately for Mike Glenn, his pet springer spaniel, Brandi, was on hand to help him after he suffered an accident commonly experienced by car owners who carry out repairs at home.

It all started when Mike, from Shawnee, Ohio, was doing some work on his Oldsmobile car at his home. The oil needed changing and a tire required fixing, so Mike raised the car on a jack and crawled underneath.

Fetching the phone had never been one of Brandi's tricks before, but the clever springer spaniel did just that when her master became trapped.

BRANDI
saves her owner

Everything was going just fine, and Mike had taken off one wheel, when the nightmare for any mechanic happened: the jack slipped. Instantly, Mike was trapped underneath his heavy car. Although the car was not crushing his body, Mike was pinned hard to the ground so there was no chance of him wriggling out. It was a desperate situation. Mike's wife, Cynthia, was out and would not be back for hours. Meanwhile the sun was about to set and, when it did, the weather would turn cold. He could not expect much help from neighbors; Mike and Cynthia live on a quiet, dark street with

houses only
every half mile or
so. Mike was worried he
might be stuck underneath his car for a very
long time. How on earth could he escape?

SIGN LANGUAGE

Help, however, was at hand. The family had a
number of pets, including Brandi the springer
spaniel. Brandi was already aware that something
was wrong and had come up to where Mike lay
and curled up next to his master. If nothing else,
Brandi could help keep Mike warm while he
figured out a plan. Then the stricken car
mechanic had an idea. Because Cynthia had a
hearing impairment, she knew some sign
language, and she had taught Brandi some signs.
Mike wondered if he could now use sign
language to persuade the dog to fetch the
phone. For a while the dog struggled to
understand what it was Mike was asking her.
Cynthia had not taught Brandi the sign language
for phone, and this behavior by Mike was all
very strange. Then Brandi suddenly realized what
her owner was asking. She dashed into the porch

of the house and picked up the phone in her
mouth. Fortunately it had a long cord and she
was able to drop it by Mike's side. Gratefully,
Mike dialed his mother-in-law for help. (He did
not dial 9-1-1 because he thought what he had
done was stupid.) However, she called the
emergency services and soon a team of
paramedics and fire fighters arrived in the
darkness to rescue him.

Fortunately, Mike was relatively unscathed
by the ordeal. As for Brandi, she had realized
Mike was in trouble and did what was necessary
to help. Exactly what made her understand what
was in Mike's mind is unclear. Interestingly, not
only had she never fetched a phone before, but
she could never be persuaded to do it again.
Brandi had only done it that one time—the
time when Mike badly needed her help.

JACK FYFE LIVED A QUIET, ALMOST RECLUSIVE LIFE at his home in Sydney, Australia. Since his wife died, the 75-year-old's only companion was Trixie, a part border collie, part kelpie. Whole days would go by without him seeing or talking to another human being.

This isolation suited Jack, who found Trixie good company, but clearly there were dangers involved in being on his own so much. One summer morning in 1999 when he awoke, Jack suddenly understood those dangers. During the night he had suffered a stroke, and was now paralyzed down one side of his body. He was unable to move out of the bed. Jack was desperately worried. His daughter had invited him to a party, so she would be expecting him for that. The trouble was, the party was not for nine days, and he might well not be missed until then. Already Jack was feeling thirsty soon after waking up. How could he survive all that time without water?

TRIXIE'S *loyalty*

A creeping feeling of panic began to envelop him, and he starting crying for help. Yet no one around could possibly hear his plaintive cries, except, of course, for Trixie. The dog had

Nobody could have believed that Jack Fyfe would survive nine days trapped at home alone, but they didn't reckon on the ingenuity of his faithful dog, Trixie.

come over to Jack when the animal realized that something was wrong. Why had her master not gotten out of bed as usual? For a while Trixie lay by Jack, as if to offer comfort by her mere presence. For his part, the old man would occasionally fall asleep, before waking up again in fear. The temperature was rising and Jack's thirst was now becoming unbearable.

IN NEED OF WATER

In desperation, he cried out, "Water, water" once more. Jack knew of course this surely could do no good. But then, out of the blue, something strange and wonderful happened. Trixie walked into the kitchen and grabbed a towel in her mouth. She then took the towel to her water bowl, soaked it in water, and then took it over to Jack's bedroom. The old man gratefully sucked the water from the towel into his mouth, savoring each drop as it trickled down his parched throat. The sheepdog repeated this act until the water bowl was empty. Then, when there was no water left, Trixie performed

the same trick with the water in the toilet bowl. This incredible behavior went on for more than a week.

Occasionally the phone would ring, or mail would drop through the mailbox. But no one came to the house. Meanwhile, each day, Trixie would take the towel and keep a regular supply of water to her ailing master. Then after nine days, and as Jack had desperately hoped, his daughter became worried when he did not attend the party. At last, she came to the house. Seeing his plight, his daughter quickly called paramedics who immediately took him to the hospital.

Once there, Jack made a slow but good recovery from his ordeal. No one doubted that but for Trixie's actions, Jack would not have made it through those nine days. How she had known what Jack's problem was and just what to do, nobody could guess. But Jack knew that in Trixie he had found the most loyal and faithful friend any man could want.

aN ANIMAL DOES NOT ALWAYS have to be classified as a pet for it to develop some kind of bond with a human. Simple acts of kindness and respect shown by people can be enough to make any animal feel it has a special link with them. So it was with Rachel and June Flynn and a remarkable gray seagull.

The two sisters shared a house near Cape Cod, New England, and enjoyed the marvelous scenery and beautiful sea views. They also took pleasure in watching the various species of wildlife that lived in abundance in that rugged terrain, and regularly fed some of the animals and birds. In particular they fed a gray seagull that seemed to return to them on a regular basis, and whom they got to know well enough to christen Nancy.

Both Rachel and June liked to take walks, although, since they were elderly, they had to be careful. Some of the paths were very precarious and there were sheer drops from the cliffs on to the beaches below. One day in 1980, Rachel, age 82, was on her own when she stumbled on one of those dangerous paths. To her horror, she found herself slipping helplessly down and over the cliff edge, tumbling down 30 feet and landing with a heavy bump on to the beach below. For a while she lay stunned, and then she began to assess what had happened. She was too hurt to move and there was no chance of calling for help, since there was no one around and the nearest house was her own, and that was a mile away. Yet without help, she believed she might die on this bleak and exposed spot.

NANCY
the seagull's
remarkable rescue

SISTER ALERTED

As Rachel began to fear the worst, she suddenly noticed a bird hovering almost above her. Looking up, she noticed it was a gray seagull and it appeared to be focusing its beady gaze on her. Could it be, thought Rachel, that this was *her* seagull, the one that she and June regularly fed? The old woman was not sure, but by

After Rachel Flynn tumbled over a cliff she feared the worst, but Nancy the tame seagull she had often fed, summoned help.

now she was desperate and called out to the bird, "Nancy, for God's sake, please get help!" At these words, the gray bird flew off.

Minutes later, June heard an unusual noise at the window in the kitchen where she was working. Looking out she saw a gray seagull flapping its wings and hitting the glass with its beak. It was a strange and almost unnerving sight, and the bird, whom June assumed was a hungry Nancy, would not fly away. The noise went on for some 15 minutes before June wondered if there was something more than mere hunger that was making the bird behave this way. June went outside, and saw Nancy fly away a short distance, but each time June approached the gull, it flew away a little more, making it look as if it was trying to make June follow. After about a mile, the gull finally

stopped and perched on the edge of a cliff. Peering over the edge, June saw immediately that Rachel was down below, and in trouble.

After calling out to reassure and calm her sister, June hurried back to the house to call the fire department, who quickly rescued Rachel. Fortunately, she had suffered no worse than bad bruising and a twisted knee, but both sisters knew that without Nancy's actions, Rachel might well have perished. As June said, "It was simply incredible the way Nancy came to the window and caused all that racket."

I N TIMES OF WAR, pets of various types have been very useful in predicting when air-raid siren warnings or enemy bombing raids are about to occur. During World War II, when German bombing raids hit many British cities and towns, cats in particular were thought to be very good at predicting when a raid was imminent. As a result, the pets were credited with saving many lives. In Leipzig, Germany, there was a parrot that was able to predict Allied air raids in 1943 up to two hours before they happened. Closer to the present day, a dog in Israel in 1991 was known to foretell the missile attack warnings before they occurred during the first Gulf War.

FRIENDSHIP
returned in WWII

One of the most remarkable and moving stories involves a stray cat during World War II. The gray tabby lived in the old medieval German city of Magdeburg. This beautiful place, which lies on the edge of the River Elbe, was one of the most bombed German cities of the war, losing even its beautiful and ancient cathedral. The tabby, whose name has not been recorded, lived as a stray in the city, probably one of many pets made homeless by the Allied bombing raids. It was befriended by a

The mysterious arrival at his house of the stray cat he had befriended was a surprise for the still sleepy German. But the tabby had come to save his life.

middle-aged German man who used to stroke it and pet it whenever he saw it near to his workplace.

A STRANGE SCRATCHING

One morning in 1944, the man was at home shaving when he heard a cat meowing loudly at his front door. When he opened it, the man was astonished to see that it was the stray cat whom he had befriended. He was surprised because this cat lived on the other side of the city near to where the man worked, and he could not believe that the animal knew where he lived. The man's puzzlement was increased by the cat's strange behavior. Normally a calm and placid animal, the cat was now meowing loudly and scratching at the man's trousers. Although he could not be sure, it seemed as though the cat was trying to get him to follow him. Perhaps it had kittens that needed a home? So, after hastily getting dressed, the man left his house and set off up the street after the stray. As they walked, the cat kept looking back as if to check that the man was still following. Eventually, about half a mile away, the cat stopped and the man looked around, still puzzled. What was it he was supposed to be looking for? Just then, they heard the unmistakable sound of RAF Lancaster bombers overhead, starting another of their surprise and deadly raids. As the man watched in horror, he saw the first of the bombs dropping from the British planes. They obliterated a row of houses, including the one he and the mysterious stray cat had just left. Touched by the man's friendliness and concern for a simple stray cat, the animal had repaid him by saving his life.

IVY & PALS
save a lost boy

I T WAS JUNE 1990 IN NEW MEXICO, and James and Angie Mann
were enjoying a break in the hills west of Albuquerque. They were
staying in a log cabin with their two-year-old son, Ernest, and the
family dog, Ivy. One afternoon, however, Ernest wandered off and was
soon missing. James and Angie immediately began looking for the little
boy, noticing that Ivy was missing too. Although they searched for two
hours, they found nothing. Desperately worried, they called in the local
sheriff and very soon a major rescue operation was underway involving
deputies, state police, volunteers, and bloodhounds. There were two main
concerns, shared by the rescue teams and James and Angie Mann alike: the
first was the temperature. Although the days were warm, the nighttime
temperatures in the hills could drop to only just above freezing at night or
in the early morning, and Ernest was wearing only light, cotton clothes.
Second, there was the possibility that Ernest and the dog had been attacked
by wild animals. The area was known for coyotes, black bears, and even
mountain lions. The search was, therefore, a race against time. By nightfall
there was still no sign of either boy or dog, and James and Angie, distraught
with anxiety, were forced to spend an awful night of waiting and
speculation. At daybreak, an even bigger search was underway involving a

military helicopter and volunteers on horseback. However, as the minutes ticked by, the rescue teams knew that hopes of finding Ernest alive were fading fast. Yet, there was still a chance.

KEEPING WARM

Later that morning, with still with no sign of Ernest, a member of the rescue team was searching through a clearing when a black dog walked out of the trees. It calmly walked up to the volunteer, gently put its jaws on the man's arms and tried to pull him slowly in one direction. The volunteer, who was experienced in the ways of animals, did not panic and realized that the dog was trying to tell him something. Together, the man and the dog walked for a short while until the rescuer was greeted by a peculiar sight. There in front of him lay the little boy, snuggled up asleep between a white dog with black spots—Ivy—and another, unknown dog.

The black dog then sat down itself next to the boy, further insulating Ernest from the morning cold. At this point, the two-year-old woke up. Clearly tired and confused, Ernest was overjoyed to see that he was safe. He announced to the equally overjoyed rescuers: "Doggies! Warm!"

The dogs had, indeed, been warm; it seems the three of them, organized by Ivy, had kept little Ernest warm through the potentially deadly cold of the night. As Ernest was carried to safety, the two unknown stray dogs casually wandered off, their job done. When danger had threatened, Ivy had known just what to do. With a little help from her friends, she had ensured that Ernest made it safely through the night.

His parents feared the worst when two-year-old Ernest went missing. But Ivy and her friends took turns keeping the young child warm through the cold night.

When Nigel Etherington decided to help the wounded wallaby he had found by the side of the road he didn't realize he would be repaid with the saving of his own life.

THERE IS AN OLD SAYING that one good turn—or deed—deserves another. This expression usually describes the relationship between two humans. But it can apply equally well to humans and animals.

Nigel Etherington was a farmer living outside the city of Perth, in Western Australia. Besides tending livestock for a living, Nigel was also something of an animal lover; in fact he was quite soft-hearted when it came to furry creatures. So it was no surprise to anyone that one night in December 1996, Nigel was a Good Samaritan to an animal in need. He had stopped his truck not far from his house after seeing something struggling by the side of the road. Getting out of his vehicle, Nigel realized that the struggling creature was a wallaby. Wallabies are members of the kangaroo family, and are generally smaller than other breeds of that marsupial. This one clearly had been hit by a passing motorist who probably had not even bothered to stop, as often happens to wallabies and kangaroos on roads in Australia. Although the Australian farmers consider

smokey
saves his savior

wallabies a pest, Nigel decided to take it home. Left out in the bush on its own, the wallaby would either be killed or die from shock and thirst. So the farmer gently lifted the stricken animal into the vehicle and drove it back to the farm—it was too weak to protest.

CLOSE ESCAPE

Once there, Nigel did what he could to care for the wallaby's injuries, and gave it some water to drink and a little food. He also knew that the best chance for the wallaby to recover was to allow it some proper rest. This would help it get over the shock of the accident. So that evening Nigel left the wounded wallaby in a comfortable spot in his bathroom. Only time would tell if the wallaby would last through the night. Meanwhile, Nigel himself went off to bed.

Nigel did not get much sleep, however. In the early hours of the morning he was abruptly woken by a ferocious thumping at his door. For a few moments Nigel tried to ignore the noise, but the thumping continued and he got up and threw open the door. What he saw stunned him. In front of him was the little wallaby, which had been thumping himself against the farmer's bedroom door for all he was worth. Behind him, Nigel could see smoke billowing through the rest of the house. An electrical fault had caused a fire in the spare room and the blaze was threatening to burn the entire house down. Nigel just had time to escape the fire, with the wallaby hopping frantically after him. Once outside, Nigel realized that the wallaby had been awakened by the smoke and discovered the fire. Although the animal could have escaped at once by itself, he had first decided to wake up Nigel, the man who had rescued him from the roadside. The farmer had no doubt about what the actions of the wallaby—now christened Smokey—had achieved. "If the wallaby hadn't woken me up I would have died," he said simply. Smokey had repaid the farmer's good turn.

across
the divide

DEATH is the ultimate punctuation mark of life. However, many humans believe it does not mark the end, but merely a new beginning. So too, do pets. The love and friendship that we share with our pets cannot simply be blotted out by death. Across that great divide pets can still communicate with those they love. Sometimes they have a message of reassurance; at other times a timely warning for us. Indeed, they can sometimes come back to save us. For the caring pet, death is truly no obstacle.

P ETS SEEM TO KNOW when someone they love has passed on, even if they are some distance away. Somehow, they can sense it. There is, for example, the remarkable story of a tomcat who belonged to a young man named Frank Pulfer from Switzerland. Frank was a ship's cook and was away for long periods, although the cat always knew when he was coming home on leave. One day the cat began wailing uncontrollably and demanded to be let into Frank's room, something he had never done before. Two days later the family was sadly informed that Frank had died during a voyage near Thailand, some 7,000 miles away. The cat began his strange behavior at the exact time that his master had passed away.

Holly had formed a special attachment to Mr. Smith. When the elderly man died, his spirit came to say goodbye to the labrador he had befriended.

HOLLY'S
final greeting

Sometimes an animal does not even have to belong to a person to be able to know what has happened to him or her. This was the case with a golden labrador named Holly. Like so many of her breed, Holly was a sharp, intelligent animal. She belonged to the Johnson family who lived in Birmingham,

England. An elderly gentleman named Mr. Smith lived close to the Johnsons. He was in his eighties and had lived in the area for many years. Mr. Smith liked to play with Holly and would sometimes bring her dog biscuits as a treat. One day he confided to the family that he had once had a dog very much like Holly, and that playing with her brought back memories of his youth.

SPECIAL FRIENDSHIP

The friendship was returned, and Holly enjoyed it whenever the old man came to visit or met her in the street. Indeed, the family soon realized they could predict when Mr. Smith would arrive, because a few minutes beforehand, Holly would stand by the front door, wagging her tail furiously and barking excitedly. She never behaved like this for anyone else.

The special relationship between Holly and the old man continued for some time. Then, in the early hours of one morning in 1995,

Carolyn and Steven Johnson were awakened by the noise of a dog barking excitedly. It was Holly. Rushing downstairs, they saw that Holly was standing next to the front door, wagging her tail and barking, just as she did when old Mr. Smith was about to call. Still half asleep, the Johnsons wondered whether, at this late hour, the elderly man was outside and in some kind of trouble. But when they opened the door, the street was empty.

It was later that morning that Carolyn and Steven heard the bad news. Apparently, Mr. Smith had become ill the previous night and was taken to a hospital, but his condition had deteriorated. He finally passed away at 3:00 that morning. The Johnsons immediately understood the significance of the time. That was when Holly had started barking and wagging her tail. The dog had been greeting her friend, Mr. Smith, one last time, before he passed away.

THERE ARE A NUMBER OF STORIES of pets who have returned from beyond the grave to help their owners. But it can also happen the other way around. An example is the story of Olga Dakin and her beloved pet Sam.

When a serious illness forced Olga to move into a hospital ward, one of the things she missed most was the company of her West Highland white terrier, Sam. Olga, a spiritualist medium from Manchester, England, was devoted to the animal and kept a photograph of the dog next to her bed. Fortunately, Olga was able to chat about her love of the terrier to one of the nurses, who shared a passion for this lovable breed and also owned one. The weeks went by, and Olga grew weaker and weaker, until one day in 1990, she sadly died. Among the many matters to be dealt with was what to do with Sam. Olga's distraught son, Gary, was very fond of his mother's dog, but he worked all day, and knew it would not be good for the animal to be left on his own for so long. So Sam went to live

sam
the terrier's
guardian angel

with someone Gary knew, Helen Rooke, who loved West Highland terriers and was sure to give the little dog a good home. Soon Sam was settled in at Helen's house in Manchester and beginning to enjoy life again. One day, however, a gate was left open and

When Sam the West Highland terrier got lost in the city, no one knew that he had his very own guardian angel to watch over him.

the inquisitive terrier managed to escape into the busy streets. Helen feared Sam might not be able to cope with the traffic near her house, and called Gary. Together the pair searched the streets nearby, but with no luck. As darkness fell, Sam was still missing, and both Helen and Gary feared the worst.

That evening, a woman was driving home through the busy streets when, out of the blue, something told her she should stop her car. Although it was raining and dark and she had been looking forward to getting home, the woman pulled her car over and got out.

SPIRITUAL GUIDANCE

What was she looking for? What strange impulse had brought her to this desolate spot? The answer came quickly. There, lying under some bushes, lay a small, white dog. The animal, a West Highland terrier, clearly had been injured by a car and lay shivering and suffering from shock by the side of the road. The young woman picked up the dog and saw from its collar tag he

was called Sam. She took the injured animal home to be warm and dry and he soon recovered. Sam even found a new friend at the house, for the woman also owned a West Highland terrier just like him. Later that evening, when she was sure Sam was okay, the woman dialed the telephone number on the collar and got hold of Helen. The woman explained briefly what had happened and a relieved Helen drove over immediately to get Sam. As the two of them chatted, Sam's rescuer explained to Helen how she had stopped and found Sam, but still could not explain just what had made her do it. Helen joked that perhaps she had somehow been guided by Sam's late owner, Olga, who was a spiritualist. At the mention of this name the young woman was taken aback. She explained that she was a nurse and she had often chatted with a patient named Olga who used to speak of her pet West Highland terrier. Perhaps, indeed, Olga had been Sam's guardian angel.

SAM WAS MAD ABOUT HORSES. Even before he could walk the young boy was fascinated by the animals that lived on his family's farm in Kansas. As he grew up the boy learned to ride and was soon able to handle most horses. But he had a particular favorite, a dark brown horse named Flash. Flash was named for a white streak that went down the front of his face. He was not the biggest of animals but he had great character and a lot of determination. Above all, he seemed to love Sam every bit as much as the boy loved the horse. The pair used to ride all

FLASH,
the horse that said good-bye

around the farm and over neighboring land, always happy in each other's company, always trusting that the one would look out for the other. Flash, though, was not getting any younger, and even Sam knew that one day he would have to get used to that sad day when he would have to say good-bye to his old friend. It was a moment he dreaded.

One winter's night in the 1920s when the snow was thick on the ground, Sam was soundly asleep in bed when something awoke him from his slumber. Listening intently in the dark, Sam could hear a loud, insistent knocking at the door. It went on for some time, and so the young boy went downstairs to investigate. He was not alone.

Flash the horse couldn't leave this world without first saying good-bye to the young boy who had been his best friend.

BLANKET OF SNOW

His father and the rest of the family had been woken by the knocking noises and were also down in the hallway. Sam and his father carefully opened the door and peered outside to see what on earth had been causing such a noise. But all they could see in the darkness was the thick white blanket of snow on the ground. There was scarcely a breath of wind, and all around them was that special soft silence that is only experienced after heavy snowfall. Sam and his father looked down at the deep snow,

expecting to see tracks or footprints of some kind, but there were none. As their eyes adjusted to the darkness, they could see that nowhere was the snow—it had fallen some hours before—disturbed in any place. It seemed that nothing or no one had come to the door that night, despite the knocking they had heard. Puzzled, but unable to solve this mystery, the family went back to bed to try and find some sleep in what remained of the night. Only Sam lay awake, wondering what it was that had made the noise.

The next morning the family were going about their normal business when Sam's father made a sad discovery. Flash was lying dead in his stable. Sam was quickly summoned to the scene, and it was soon established by the local veterinarian that the elderly horse had died peacefully, and without pain in the night.

Suddenly Sam and the rest of the family realized what they had all heard the night before. The faithful horse had known he was dying. But death was not going to stop him saying a last farewell to his friend and master, the boy who had been his constant companion for so many years. In the depth of his grief, Sam found comfort in the knowledge that Flash's spirit had come to say good-bye.

IT IS THE NATURAL URGE OF A LOYAL AND FAITHFUL PET to want to help its master or mistress, and sometimes not even death can stop this from happening. For example, in 1946, Norma Kresgal from New York City, befriended an injured dog called Corky who could not bark properly. The grateful Corky then spent many happy years with Norma's family. One night, two years after Corky had died, Norma was awakened to hear an odd, but familiar sound: Corky's distinctive barking. She also noticed her apartment was on fire, and was able to escape thanks to Corky's warning.

An even more striking tale concerns Ruth Whittlesey and her dog Nigel. Back in 1940, Ruth, the wife of a church minister, was working as a superintendent at a hospital in Hawthorne, California. It was a rewarding job, but physically and emotionally demanding too, and often meant working late hours. One night, Ruth received a call at home requesting her to go to the hospital. A patient was dying and she was asked to be with him and comfort him in his last moments. It was part of her job, and so Ruth wasted no time in getting ready to make her way to the hospital. She lived close enough to walk to work, although it was not the most reassuring of journeys; there were few lights and her route took her along some dark roads. That night, however, as she hurried to the hospital, Ruth had things on her mind other than her personal safety.

Nigel the fiercely loyal guard dog was so determined to protect his mistress Ruth, he even came back from the grave to save her when she was threatened in the street one dark night.

RESCUER NIGEL
back from the grave

HASTY RETREAT

As Ruth strode along an unlit area of street, she was alarmed to see a dark-colored car pulling up nearby. Ruth could not see everything clearly, but she could make out two stockily built men in the car. Unnerved, and unwilling to take any chances, she ran off down the street, but the car followed, easily keeping up with her. Now Ruth was getting very frightened, fearing that her life could be in danger. Alone, she would be little match for two large men.

Just then a reassuring figure sped into view. It was Nigel, Ruth's chocolate labrador, and a powerful and imposing animal. Nigel immediately placed himself between his mistress and the car. The two men, who had shown every sign of getting out of the vehicle, had a quick look at this massive hound and decided to make a hasty retreat. As the car drove quickly off, Nigel trotted alongside Ruth until they reached a safe area nearer the hospital, and then he too disappeared. It was not until a few moments later, after Ruth had regained her composure, that she realized how strange it had been that her dog had turned up like that. After all, as she and her husband both well knew, Nigel had passed away some months before.

SOME PETS FIND IT HARD TO LET GO. Although death has separated them from the family they loved, they continue to behave as before, perhaps hoping they can be reunited with their owner. In Japan, there was a famous dog called Hachi, who used to walk with his master to a railway station in Tokyo to see him off to work. At 5 P.M. Hachi would wait at the same station to greet his master. One day Hachi's master did not turn up at 5 P.M., because he had died at work. This did not deter the dog, however. He continued to arrive at the station at 5 P.M. every working day. Hachi did this until his

JOCK'S
warning

own death, some ten years later. Another pet, who found it hard to let go, was a Scottish terrier named Jock. Jock lived with Paul and Jennifer Smith in their New England home in the 1960s. It was a busy household: the couple worked together on restoration projects, and in addition, they had two delightful and lively daughters, Amy and Francesca, to look after. Jock, too, was very much a part of the family. He seemed to see himself as their guardian, and was a very alert and effective watchdog. What the little terrier lacked in stature, he more than made up for in character and determination. If something unusual occurred, or a stranger arrived, Jock was sure to know instantly, and he would let people know with his sharp little barks. It was a role the dog happily carried out for many years.

The warning barks from Jock the terrier saved the Smith family from almost certain death in a house fire. Yet, the lovable family pet had passed away some months before.

AWAKENED BY BARKING

One night Paul and Jennifer were especially tired. They had been working together on a large project that had involved long and exhausting hours. Francesca also had been sick with a bad cough, so neither of them had enjoyed a good night's sleep for days. This evening, though, they sank contentedly into a long, deep, and much-needed sleep.

However, in the early hours of the morning, Jennifer was awakened by the sound of Jock barking in their bedroom. Soon after, Paul was awake too, and in the darkness they could make out the unmistakable dark, barking figure of the dog at the end of the bed. However, before Paul or Jennifer could say anything to Jock, they noticed something else too: the smell of smoke. They both leapt out of bed and on to the landing, where they saw flames flickering amid the billowing smoke. Frantically, the couple rushed to the girls' bedrooms, grabbed them, and ran down the stairs to safety. Although neighbors called the firefighters, it was too late to save the house, which was completely destroyed. But the important thing was that all the family had escaped. As for Jock, he did not perish in the fire either for the simple reason that he had already died of old age some months before. In life, Jock had looked after the safety of the family. Now Paul and Jennifer knew that even in death, he was still doing the same.

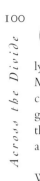

ONE NIGHT IN JULY 1962, William and Mina Miles were returning from a party to their home in Yarmouth, Maine, when they noticed an animal lying motionless in the middle of the road near their house. Mina had a bad feeling about the discovery, as the animal's coloring looked very familiar. Sure enough, when William got out of their car and saw the animal, he realized it was their pet cat Streaky, who clearly had been hit and killed by a car that evening.

The death of Streaky was a particular blow to William and Mina. Streaky had recently given birth to a litter of four kittens who were now without a mother. They also were still upset that Streaky's own mother, a ginger cat called Hoppy, had disappeared more than a month before and had not been seen since. Had mother and daughter shared the same fate?

Early the next morning William went down to the cellar where Streaky's kittens were living, wondering what on earth the family could do with them. Would they have to be given away, or worse? Suddenly, in the

Somehow Hoppy the cat knew when her daughter had been killed and that her kittens needed the kind of help only she could give.

GRANDMOTHER
cat's preternatural powers

cellar window, he saw a familiar sight. It was Streaky's mother, Hoppy, who, despite their fears, was alive and well. The older cat was trying to get into the basement, and William quickly let her in through the window. Immediately she made a beeline straight for the hungry kittens, her grand-kittens. William saw that Hoppy also recently had kittens, which meant she was able to feed this new litter as well. It seemed the perfect solution: Hoppy could look after Streaky's litter as well as her own.

BREATHLESS CHASE

Yet no sooner were William and Mina counting their blessings, when Hoppy disappeared again. Where had she gone? William decided to follow her. After a breathless chase through woods and scrubland, William finally tracked down Hoppy. She had gone inside a shed next to a house about a mile away from the Miles' own home. This house belonged to the Nixon family who had a story to tell about the cat William called Hoppy. Back in May, the cat had just arrived at the house, and a month later had given birth to a litter of a five kittens. They were in the shed.

A devoted mother, Hoppy had barely left the kittens for a second. Not, that is, until the previous night. Hoppy had been behaving strangely, meowing and crying as if she wanted to be let out. Early the next morning the Nixons had finally given in to Hoppy's plaintive cries and opened the door. Ignoring her own kittens' cries, she had dashed off into the distance. Now she had returned with William Miles in hot pursuit.

The curious story was now becoming clearer to both families. Hoppy had started acting oddly in the Nixon's house at about 9:00 on that evening, about the time the Miles family calculated Streaky was knocked down and killed. It seems Hoppy must have sensed that her daughter had died and that her kittens would be helpless, unless she came to the rescue. How could she have known about her daughter's death a mile away? Nobody could guess. But thanks to Hoppy's actions, her daughter's kittens had been given the chance for a happy life.

COCKY ROBERtS'
last call

IGNACY PADEREWSKI (1860–1941) WAS A REMARKABLE MAN. He was an outstanding statesman in his native Poland, an accomplished composer, a fine orator, and above all a brilliant pianist. His popularity was greater nowhere than in the United States where he gave many acclaimed concert performances. In 1932, President Franklin D. Roosevelt even described Paderewski as a "modern immortal," such was his genius and profile. For his part, the pianist simply loved the United States, a country that he regarded as his second home.

It is not surprising that such a remarkable man should have had a remarkable pet. That pet was a parrot called Cocky Roberts. Cocky Roberts was by no means a shy or subdued kind of parrot. For example, the parrot insisted that he be present whenever his master was practicing the piano. If, for any reason, the parrot was kept out of the practice room, he made a huge fuss. The bird would knock on the door with his powerful beak, shouting out, "Cocky Roberts let me in!" This usually did the trick with the kind-hearted Paderewski.

Once inside the rehearsal room, Cocky Roberts would be quiet enough, although he did have the habit of sitting on the piano pedal and moving up and down in rhythm with the music. However, at the end of the practice Cocky would pass judgment on the quality of his brilliant master's playing. As a rule the bird would call out, "How beautiful" or some other expression of praise. Every now and again, however, Cocky Roberts would announce that the musician had been, "lousy, lousy." To his great credit, Paderewski admitted that the parrot was usually fairly accurate in his comments!

CLOSE BOND

A close bond developed between this great man and his remarkable bird, which made it hard for both of them if the pianist had to leave the parrot at home during concert tours.

During one tour of the United States, Paderewski left Cocky Roberts behind in his villa in Switzerland. The pianist was staying in New York City one night when he had a vivid dream involving his pet. Paderewski dreamed that the parrot was calling out to him in his familiar, harsh voice. When he awoke, the great pianist said he felt a profound sense of emptiness. Somehow he just knew that Cocky Roberts was dead. The news came ten days later that an unfortunate accident had occurred at Paderewski's Swiss home. The parrot had inadvertently been left outside overnight in the freezing-cold temperatures of that Alpine country. The morning after, Cocky Roberts had been found dead outside the villa, his body as stiff as a board. Paderewski was not surprised to learn that the parrot had died on the very night that he had dreamed of him in New York. The bird obviously had been saying good-bye to the great man for the last time. As Paderewski was later to remark, "That bird had a soul."

The remarkable bond between parrot Cocky Roberts and his master continued even after the bird's death, when he mysteriously appeared in the piano virtuoso's dreams.

J OE BENSON WAS A SPIRITUAL LEADER among the Goshute Indians whose people traditionally had lived in and around the Great Salt Lake Desert. One day in the 1950s, Joe came across an emaciated stray puppy and decided to adopt it. He saw that within this weak-looking little puppy there was a strong life force, and slowly nursed the little animal to good health. Before long the dog, whom Joe named Sky, had grown into a healthy and powerful adult German shepherd dog. The two went everywhere together, and as Joe grew older and his sight failed, Sky

When Joe Benson returned to fetc his dog Sky, it didn't matter that the spiritual leader had been dead for some days. His spirit and his dog strode away into the horizon.

man's spirit
returned to collect his dog

looked out for his master, making sure he did not fall. It was as if the dog was repaying the kindness the old man had shown him all those years ago.

Soon Joe knew that his time was close and announced to his wife, Mabel, that he was about to die. His family gathered to be with him, and insisted that he go into the hospital. The doctors and nurses, however, realized there was little they could do for Joe, and wisely discharged him so he could be at home on his own land when the end arrived.

REUNITED

Joe finally died early in 1963 and his family and friends organized a fine funeral befitting such a respected member of their community. Then, after the official mourning was over and Joe's spirit was thought to have passed over, the guests departed. Mabel and Sky were left on their own to mourn their loss.

A few days later, Mabel was standing at her kitchen window when, in the distance, she saw someone approaching the house. She went into the kitchen to put on some coffee for the visitor, and when she looked up again, she could see who that figure was. It was her husband Joe, and he was standing in the doorway. Mabel, who was well acquainted with her people's ways, explained patiently to Joe that he was now dead and had no place with the living. Her late husband indicated his agreement and said he had briefly returned for one reason only. "I came for

my dog," he explained simply. By this time Sky was in the room, wagging his tail in delight at the reappearance of his master. Joe then asked Mabel for Sky's leash, which she carefully handed to him. The old man then put the leash on the expectant dog, and together the pair walked out of the house, down the path, and disappeared over the side of a hill. Mabel ran after the two of them, but they were nowhere to be seen. Joe and Mabel's daughter, Arvilla, who lived next door, also witnessed the incident. She, too, went to the top of the hill, but both her father and Sky had vanished into thin air. Neither man, dog, nor leash was ever seen again. Joe and his treasured dog Sky had been reunited forever.

GOLDEN RETRIEVER, COOKIE MONSTER, was a special dog in Lori Krug's life. Lori, a civil servant from Edmonton, Alberta, understood that her canine friend was a true free spirit, who enjoyed life to the fullest. Boisterous, full of fun, and endlessly enthusiastic, Cookie was simply a joy to have around the house. When Lori took on two more dogs, Echo and Zoey, Cookie looked after them, showed them around, and made sure they fitted smoothly into family life. Cookie did not even mind going to the veterinarian; in fact, she even seemed to enjoy it. This was just as well, because with her lively and inquisitive nature, Cookie sometimes got herself into a bit of trouble; for example, with bees. But mostly she enjoyed good health, until old age took its toll.

Lori knew something was seriously wrong during Christmas in 1998. The dog did not rip open her presents as usual and barely touched her special Christmas dinner. A trip to the veterinarian confirmed the worst. Cookie had developed cancer of the spleen, which had in turn led to internal bleeding. Unfortunately, nothing could be done to save her. So for one last time, Lori took Cookie back home to say good-bye to

COOKIE'S
final wishes

The energetic retriever Cookie didn't want to be remembered after her death as a pile of ashes, so she made sure that not all of her owner's tribute photographs came out.

her parents and her canine friends, Zoey and
Echo. Then it was back to the veterinarian's
office to have the much-loved golden retriever
painlessly put to sleep.

DREAM MESSAGE

For some days, Lori was too shaken with grief
to do much, although the presence of her other
two dogs was a great comfort. Then, about a
week after Cookie's death, Lori went to the
veterinarian's office to collect her dog's ashes,
which were in an urn. Determined to remember
Cookie in every way possible, Lori took six
photographs of the urn surrounded by flowers
she had received from family and friends. This,
she thought, would be one way to remember
their beloved Cookie.

That night, however, the golden retriever
appeared to Lori in a dream and was talking to
her. Cookie was telling Lori that she did not
want to be remembered as a pile of ashes in an
urn, but as a living, vibrant animal. Coming after

that day's events, it was a curious dream, but
Lori was not sure how seriously to take it.

Some weeks later, Lori's mother took the
roll of film that contained those last urn pictures
to be developed. Her mother told Lori that the
photographs were all fine—at least, those that
had come out. When Lori examined the
photographs herself she saw what her mother
meant. A photo of Cookie taken just before her
final trip to the veterinarian had come out fine,
as had some later shots of Zoey and Echo. But
none of the six photographs of Cookie's ashes in
the urn had come out at all. Not one. Lori
knew she had taken those photographs exactly
the same way as she had the others. So what had
gone wrong? Then she remembered the dream.
Had Cookie gotten her own way about how she
wanted to be remembered? As Lori says,
"Somehow, I don't know how, I think Cookie
managed to do something to those photographs.
It wasn't spooky; I just found it very moving.
She was a very special dog."

HERBERT J. REBHAN GRADUATED FROM VETERINARY SCHOOL in 1984, and enlisted as a volunteer in the Peace Corps. The young American had a daunting task ahead of him. He was assigned to the central African country of Malawi and had been given the job of district veterinary officer for the Thyolo district. This involved Herbert covering hundreds of miles in the southern areas of Thyolo and Mulanji, with just a small motorbike to transport him. The young veterinarian's job was to supervise more than 20 veterinary technicians in the area and to have overall responsibility for the health of the many cattle, sheep, and other domesticated animals that lived there. However, most of the drugs he had at his disposal were out of date. Yet, he was soon relishing the challenges that this assignment gave him.

About a month after he had started work, an elderly man came to visit Herbert's office. His name was Dr. Mzimba, and he

DOCtOLa
and the dogs who repaid his help

was a medicine man; that is to say a healer, wise man, and spiritual leader. The old man had been traveling all day from his village by bus and foot to reach the veterinarian. With

When Herbert J. Rebhan saved two puppies from illness he gained two strong dogs as his protectors.

him were six very sick puppies. Dr. Mzimba explained that he cared very deeply for these little animals and had foreseen that at least some of them would do great things in the future. However, his healing powers were limited to people, not animals, so he wondered if the young veterinarian could save them. Herbert agreed to try, explaining that they would need round-the-clock care, and that they would have to remain with him. Dr. Mzimba assented, and set off on the eight-hour trek back to his village.

DOCTOLA'S PROTECTORS

The six puppies were in bad shape and Herbert knew it was unlikely that any of them would survive. He used antibiotics and homemade electrolyte solution on the animals, but to little effect. One by one the tiny puppies began to succumb to their illness. Soon, after six days, only two were left. That night Herbert went to bed not expecting the remaining pups to make it through the night. But to his surprise and delight they were not only alive in the morning, but they also showed signs of being hungry.

Soon, after regular meals, the once painfully thin puppies began to fill out and become fine young animals. They were both distinctly marked: one was black with four white paws and a large white mark in the shape of a star on its front; the other was mostly brown with a white patch on its face, while both of them had prominent ridgebacks (a ridge along the spine with parallel crowns of hair growing in opposite directions).

When Dr. Mzimba returned to see the veterinarian more than two weeks later, he was delighted to see that two of the puppies had not only survived, but were also thriving. Before he took them home, the old medicine man gave Herbert the honor of naming the two animals. The veterinarian chose Bozo for the black pup and Skippy for the other, both the names of dogs he had owned as a youth. Dr. Mzimba said the two puppies would never forget Herbert's kindness to them and that one day they would be sure to repay it.

The veterinarian saw the two dogs regularly over the next 18 months. Every month or so he

would take a tour of his area on his motorbike, and usually would drop in on Dr. Mzimba's village. The two dogs, who had grown into large, powerful animals, always greeted him with great delight. Sometimes, they needed treatment from him. The medicine man explained that the pair were the largest and fiercest dogs in the village and that they protected the people's livestock from marauding hyenas and jackals. Inevitably, they would suffer cuts and bruises in these brutal encounters.

On one memorable occasion, Bozo and Skippy killed a leopard that had been preying on village livestock. This fight left the dogs close to death, and Herbert was forced to stitch up their wounds and give them antibiotics. A grateful Dr. Mzimba pointed out that this was the second time the American had saved the lives of the two dogs. He told the young man, whom he always called Doctola, "From this time on, Doctola, they will be your protectors. I have seen it."

Months passed and Herbert once more found himself heading for the village on one of his routine trips. This time it was the rainy season, and the wet conditions made the muddy track treacherous for his small motorbike. Time after time Herbert slithered and fell off in the wet mud. Then, not far from the village, his single headlight beam picked out the unmistakable shape of a hyena on the track ahead. Normally, a hyena would have turned tail and run off in these circumstances, but this one showed no sign of budging in the darkness. Then Herbert saw why. The blank stare in the animal's eyes and the blood and saliva dripping from its mouth were clear enough signs that the hyena had rabies.

KINDNESS RETURNED

Herbert knew he was in trouble. The thick, heavy mud meant that it would be nearly impossible to ride away on his bike, and the path was too narrow for him to turn around. As the

hyena advanced menacingly, its jaws open, and making a terrible, mocking, laughing sound, the veterinarian decided he would have to run for it and hoped the rabid animal would attack his bike instead. Just then, as Herbert prepared to flee for his life, two large animals appeared, one on either side of him. They were Bozo and Skippy. The two animals looked in prime health as they faced up to do battle with the hyena. The fight was long and bloody, but when it was over the hyena lay dead on the ground. Their work done, the dogs vanished.

Herbert rushed as fast as he could into the village to find Dr. Mzimba's house. Surely the dogs would be injured, as a rabid animal had bitten them. They would need his urgent attention. Bozo and Skippy had just saved his life; now it was the vet's turn to save theirs. He reached the old man's hut and hurriedly explained what had just happened. Dr. Mzimba showed little reaction, then asked the

veterinarian to follow him. "I'll show you the dogs," he said. The medicine man went to the back of the hut and pointed to two graves. They belonged to Bozo and Skippy, he explained. A few days before, the dogs had fought off a pack of hyenas that had threatened the village cattle. The dogs had won, but it had been at a terrible cost to themselves. They had died of their injuries soon afterward.

Herbert was distraught and confused. He insisted that he *had* seen Bozo and Skippy just now, and that they *had* rescued him from the rabid hyena. The two dogs were very distinctive; it would have been impossible for him to have mistaken them. Dr. Mzimba sat down next to him and reassured the Doctola that he believed his story. "I told you that someday the dogs would return your kindness," said the old man. "They will always protect you."

chapter five

SEEING
the
future

Of all the marvels that pets perform, there is one quality that is the most mysterious of all: their ability to see into the future. Whether they are foretelling natural disasters, predicting terrible accidents, or simply predicting the results of a ball game, pets seem to have a spooky sense of what lies ahead. Some cultures use animals to warn them when a devastating earthquake may be about to strike. Perhaps we should all learn to have a healthy respect for the foresight of our animal companions.

SURELY ONE OF THE MOST EXTRAORDINARY DOGS to have lived in modern times was Missie, the Boston terrier. During the 1960s, Missie became something of a celebrity because of her great knowledge and remarkable ability to know details about people. She also could predict the future.

Although Missie was to have a long and fantastically interesting life, she was in fact lucky to have lived at all. Her mother had given birth to three pups when she developed severe pains. A veterinarian had to operate and found the tiny form of Missie tucked up in her mother's rib cage. The terrier was given to Mildred Probert, from Denver, Colorado, a retired floral designer who often looked after animals that had endured a tough start to life. She quickly formed a bond with Missie, who had two main physical characteristics: she was very small, even for a Boston terrier, and had very striking cobalt-blue eyes.

The terrier lived a fairly normal life for a pet dog, and it was not until she was nearly five years old that her unusual abilities were discovered.

missie,
the clairvoyant
Boston terrier

The outcome of presidential elections, the date of the moon landings, and the gender of future babies were to name but a few of Missie's incredible predictions.

Mildred was talking to a woman who had a three-year-old son, and who was trying to encourage the little boy to talk and give his age. "Three, say three," she urged gently. But instead of the boy answering, it was Missie who barked three times. Amused, Mildred then asked the dog how old Missie was—and she barked four times. Perhaps expecting to trick the dog, she then asked Missie how old she would be next week. This time the dog barked five times. It was true that her birthday was the following week.

PREDICTIONS

This was just the beginning for Missie. As Mildred began to explore her pet's abilities, she discovered that the little terrier could spell and do arithmetic. On one occasion, for example, using her own alphabetical code, she barked out the difference in spelling between the two words "marry" and "merry." That was not all; Missie apparently knew things that Mildred and other people who were present did not. For example, she could predict accurately how many coins or keys a person had in a bag. Very often, not even

the person knew the answer, but on later inspection Missie was always right. She also once bemused a newspaper reporter by barking out his social security number, something even the reporter had forgotten, and a number Mildred could not possibly have known. When a skeptical local doctor declared that he could not really believe in Missie's supposed powers, the dog responded by barking out his private home telephone number. He confessed that this was a number that no one except he could know, since he never gave it out.

At a party, a woman decided to test Missie's powers by holding up a pack of cards one by one. Only the woman knew which card it was she held. Missie and the rest of the guests only saw the back of the cards. One by one Missie barked out which card was being held up, and one by one the woman turned them over to show that Missie was correct. Remarkably, Missie had never even seen a deck of cards up to that moment.

The most startling gift that the terrier possessed, however, was her ability to see the future. It started in 1964 when she predicted that Lyndon Johnson would beat Barry Goldwater in the U.S. presidential elections, which was correct. She went on to predict that Richard Nixon would one day be president of the United States, which also came true, although after the dog's death. She continued to predict a whole range of other elections, both major and minor, with startling accuracy.

But her soothsaying was not restricted to politics. She predicted moon landings, the date of the end of the 1966 New York transit strike, and even the outcome of a series of earth tremors around Denver. In that same year, she also predicted the outcome of baseball's World Series, including the correct score—nine months in advance. The terrier also predicted the results of major football games. Other predictions at the time included the date of the resumption of the Paris Peace Talks, and their outcome, and the return of the Colorado National Reserve from Vietnam.

On a much more personal level, Missie was able to predict the birth of babies. Furthermore, not only did she correctly foresee their gender, but also their exact weight and precise time of birth. Often these predictions contradicted medical expectations at the time.

Another of Missie's abilities was to know the correct time. If Mildred asked her what the time was, the terrier always got it right, regardless of whether there was a clock in the room. A friend even made Missie a little clock on which the dog could change the hands to show the correct time. Interestingly, she always moved the hands on the clock clockwise, never counter clockwise.

FINAL PREDICTION

In addition to these gifts, Missie also had some more down-to-earth—although odd—traits as a dog. She adored the color pink, even though

dogs have poor color perception, and especially pink chocolates, and she slept in pink pajamas. Missie also liked everything to be in its correct place, and would get very upset if anyone moved one of her favorite toys, in particular her beloved little stuffed dog, or a piece of furniture. The terrier was also very fussy about food, insisting on being hand fed and refusing to eat out of dog bowls. Throughout her life, Missie never really got along with other dogs.

On one occasion, and against Mildred's wishes, Missie was asked to predict a man's death. This man, Mr. Kincaid, had stomach cancer, and doctors feared he might only last a few more months. Missie indicated he would live another two years and would die on April 4, 1967. The man did so, but not from cancer; he died from accidental gunshot wounds.

Then one day in May 1966, Missie predicted her own death. The terrier kept barking out the number eight to Mildred, even though this was not the time. When Mildred

asked what the correct time was, Missie got it right, but then barked eight again. She did this half a dozen times or more. Later that evening Missie choked on a piece of food and died. The time was exactly 8 P.M. Some time later, Mildred noticed the little toy clock that the friend had given Missie. Its hands pointed to 8:00.

The terrier's body was buried in the backyard, and her favorite pink flowers, petunias, were planted on her grave. Amazingly, the flowers continued to bloom all through winter despite the snow and ice. It was a remarkable end to a remarkable life.

Redsy loved to join his master on fishing trips. This time however the red setter's acute sense of impending danger and his refusal to board the boat saved both their lives.

aNIMALS SEEM TO HAVE A WAY OF KNOWING when bad weather or natural disasters are about to strike before humans do. In 1976, for example, a golden retriever called Lisa began barking at a British embassy building in Beijing. Her barking awoke second secretary Richard Margolis, who was looking after her. Convinced the dog knew something was wrong, Margolis roused other embassy staff who fled the building just before a massive earthquake struck near the Chinese capital.

In Kansas a cat gave birth to kittens in a barn, but a few days later inexplicably began removing them laboriously, one by one, to a neighbor's farm. When she had finished, the barn was flattened by a tornado, while the neighbor's place was untouched.

Another remarkable weather prediction was made by Redsy, a red setter. Redsy was a strong-willed and adventurous dog who belonged to New England fisherman William H. Montgomery. Redsy liked nothing more than to be out on the boat with her master, feeling the sea breeze on her face and the movement of the ocean below her paws.

REDSY
predicts a fishing trip disaster

HURRICANE WARNING

One day, William decided to take his boat out to fish for flounder. He prepared his boat in readiness for the trip, and examined the sky to see what the weather might be like. There wasn't a cloud to be seen, and there was little more than a breeze to disturb the calm surface of the sea. William also looked at the other fishing boats that were already making their way toward the popular flounder banks to start work. He knew he needed to move quickly if he wanted to take advantage of the good fishing the day promised.

Impatient to go, and with his boat ready, William whistled for Redsy to join him on board. Normally it was so automatic for Redsy to leap aboard at this signal that the fisherman barely took any notice of the dog. This time, though, it was different. Redsy stood on the dock barking loudly, and she refused to get on board the boat. William whistled again, and then gave her a few words of command, but still the setter adamantly refused to budge. The fisherman was troubled. He was eager to get out fishing, but he also had been with Redsy long enough to have a healthy respect for her sixth sense. He took one more look at the sky. Could it be that his dog knew something about the weather that he did not? William decided to take no chances, and stayed ashore.

For the rest of his life he would be glad he had taken heed of Redsy's warning. Within an hour of his scheduled departure, an unexpected storm started to make its way in from the ocean, bringing devastation in its wake. It was the hurricane of 1938, the so-called Long Island Express, which claimed about 600 lives and destroyed more than 2,500 boats and nearly 9,000 houses. The wind speeds topped 120 mph with gusts reaching 186 mph. Thanks to Redsy's warning, William Montgomery did not have to face this terrifying hurricane at sea.

B Y ANY STANDARDS, Chris was an exceptionally talented dog. A part-beagle, mixed-breed, Chris was an active, even hyperactive, dog who lived with George and Marion Woods in Rhode Island in the 1950s. He had been given to the Woods family when he was about two years old, and they had done their best to calm

CHRIS'
amazing
predictions

down this rather impulsive, although lovable, pet. Until he was about five years old, Chris lived the normal, everyday life of any similar dog in his situation. However, one day everything changed. A guest had arrived with a dog that was apparently so smart it could spell out its own name and count up to ten. As a joke, Marion Woods turned to Chris and asked *her* pet if he could tell them what two plus two equaled. To everyone's amazement, Chris calmly touched Marion's arm with his paw four times. Chris' hitherto hidden gift soon became obvious. The dog could perform simple arithmetic and learned the alphabet, and in this way he began to communicate with people. For example, Chris would spell out his thoughts about cats, whom he considered "d-u-m-b." He also expressed similar views about dogs he did not like. Chris could also answer "yes" and "no" to questions in the same way, and would even confess if he had been naughty.

CELEBRITY DOG

The pet's antics amazed friends and family alike, and it was not long before he attracted the attention of the media. In the 1950s, Chris became something of a celebrity dog, appearing on TV shows and raising money for animal charities with his performances. Chris' abilities also were studied by scientists, including his arithmetic and spelling skills, and his ability to "read" someone's mind. This was done by scientists looking at cards with different images on them, and the dog having to indicate which image he

Chris' many talents made him something of a celebrity among his friends. Even the media took notice of this remarkable dog.

thought they were looking at. The results indicated that Chris had an uncanny ability to know what was in a person's mind.

Perhaps the most striking gift that Chris showed was his ability to predict the future. One day a neighbor asked him which horse might win a certain race that was taking place the next day. The dog dutifully tapped out who he thought the winner would be, and the woman took down the name of the horse and placed a bet on it. To her great delight, it won. The dog's horse-racing predictions were soon in demand.

This gift for knowing the future also had its more poignant side. Chris had suffered for a while from a heart condition and, by the late 1950s, was not in the best of health. He was asked to predict when he would die, and Chris did not hesitate to give an answer. The dog tapped out the date, June 10, 1962. In fact Chris was to get this date wrong by one day. This bright, lovable dog instead died on June 9, 1962, the end of an extraordinary life.

IF A PET SEEMS TO BE WARNING US OF SOMETHING that is about to happen, we might do well to take heed. That was certainly the case with Josef Becker, who went for a quiet drink at his local pub in the charming German town of Saarlouis, close to the border of France. Josef took his Alsatian, Strulli, with him, but the dog was far from at ease. Although Strulli had been inside the bar many times before, he was whimpering and howling, and trying to drag Josef outside. Josef tried putting Strulli outside, but the dog found a way back in and continued his uncharacteristic behavior. Realizing he would get no peace if he stayed, Josef reluctantly left the pub with the dog and headed home. Minutes later the building collapsed, killing nine people. By eventually heeding his dog's warning Josef probably had saved his life.

Not everyone is as fortunate as Josef and Strulli, however. In World War I a British naval officer was based in Harwich on the east coast of England. He lived there with his wife and his pet Airedale dog; unfortunately none of their names have been recorded. At the time, the young lieutenant was

aIredaLe's
sense of tragedy

serving on board a minesweeper, a vessel whose job it was to keep the shipping lanes

The young naval officer took no notice of his Airedale's uncharacteristic behavior as he boarded his ship; unfortunately his dangerous mission would be his last.

off the British coast free from German mines. It was dangerous but vital work, and the stoic young officer took the perils of his mission in his stride.

DANGEROUS MISSIONS

Before he set sail, the officer's wife and the Airedale usually went to the dock to say good-bye. It was a comfort for the man to see both the woman he loved and his faithful dog when he set off on his missions. One day, however, the Airedale was in a very strange mood. All that morning the dog had behaved in an agitated and unusual manner. Then, when they got to the dock, the pet's behavior became even more odd. He refused to be patted good-bye by the officer and grabbed hold of the officer's trouser leg with his teeth. For several minutes he tried to grab hold of any part of his master's uniform he could to drag him away from the ship. The officer, though, was a calm, unflappable sort of man, and just shrugged off the dog's antics. Besides, he had his duty to perform, so, after kissing his wife good-bye, the lieutenant walked on board and got ready for the work ahead.

That same night, the Airedale suddenly began a piteous wailing, which lasted for some time. Later, the officer's wife learned that the ship had been lost at sea that night, and that all lives had been lost. It was estimated the ship had gone down at about the time the Airedale had begun to howl. The dog had foreseen his master's tragic fate, but had been unable to stop his death. Now all he could do was mourn him.

SKIPPER'S
lottery win

CATS SEEM TO HAVE AN AFFINITY FOR GAMES. Take, for example, the strange story of Willie the cat from Cincinnati. Willie, it seems, had a thing about bingo. Like most cats, Willie was usually fairly casual about times. But Monday nights were different. Every Monday at 7:30 P.M., this cat would leave home, pad across town, and go to the same hospital. Once there, and at 7:45 P.M. precisely, he would sit on the windowsill of the nurses' dining room and watch a group of women start to play bingo. Then at 9:45 P.M., when the game was over, he would quietly make his way back home again. Willie got no food from anyone at the bingo, nor did he meet any other cats, so why did he go? The strangest thing, however, was just how Willie knew when it was Monday, and how he knew when it was 7:30 P.M.

LOTTERY LUCK

Skipper, the cat, also became involved in a game, although in his case the result was more lucrative for his owners. Skipper belonged to Linda and Gayle McManamon, who live in the historic Texas city of Galveston, which lies on the edge of the Gulf of Mexico.

Skipper had always been a very likeable cat and popular with the family. But it would be fair to say that he was also a fairly ordinary, unremarkable kind of animal. That is, until one fateful evening in 1996. Gayle and Linda were relaxing in front of the television after a hard day's work. Their little cat was also in the room, playing idly on the floor, as cats do. On this particular occasion, Skipper was playing with the family's lottery shaker. (This is a simple little gadget that can be used to select lottery numbers when people cannot think of any other way.) Gayle and Linda were taking little notice of their cat, but Gayle did manage to have a quick look at what Skipper was doing. It was then that he noticed that Skipper seemed to have chosen six lottery numbers.

Neither Linda nor Gayle had had much luck with the lottery, whether they used the shaker or not. But now their cat had come up with a combination. Maybe it was worth a try? Gayle thought so and wrote down the numbers. What had they got to lose? The next morning Linda went out to buy the family's weekly lottery tickets as usual, but this time she was armed with Skipper's special set of numbers.

The next day Linda was at work when a colleague told her that in the previous night's drawings the winner had been someone from Galveston. Linda was excited. Could it be her? She called Gayle, who had just realized what happened. All of Skipper's six numbers had been drawn the night before. It was hard to believe, but their little cat had just won Linda and Gayle $3.7 million.

When Skipper got hold of the McManamon family's lottery shaker, he gave them a set of numbers which would change their lives forever.

INDEX

RESOURCES

FURTHER READING

Bardens, Dennis. *Psychic Animals*. London: Sphere Books, 1989.

Gaddis, V. and M. *The Strange World of Animals and Pets*. New York: Cowles Book Company, 1970.

Schul, Bill. *The Psychic Power of Animals*. London: Coronet Books, 1978.

Sheldrake, Rupert. *Dogs That Know When Their Owners Are Coming Home*. London: Arrow Books, 1999.

Steiger, Brad and Sherry Jansen. *Dog Miracles*. Massachusetts: Adams Media Corporation, 2001.

Sutton, John. *Psychic Pets – Supernatural True Stories of Paranormal Pets*. London: Bloomsbury, 1997.

Trapman, Captain A. H. *The Dog, Man's Best Friend*. London: Hutchinson & Co., 1929.

von Kreisler, Kristen. *Beauty in the Beasts*. New York: Tarcher/Putnam, 2002.

Wylder, Joseph. *Psychic Pets – The Secret World of Animals*. London: J. M. Dent & Sons, 1980.

USEFUL WEB SITES

www.psychics.co.uk/psychicpets/homepage.html
(for information on psychic pets)

www.psychicworld.net
(for psychic tests to perform on your pets)

www.sheldrake.org
(for more detailed information on Rupert Sheldrake's experiments with telepathy)

CREDITS

Quarto would like to thank and acknowledge the following for supplying pictures reproduced in this book:

Horsepix p11 top right, p26 top center, bottom right, p27 top right, p78 top right, p79 bottom, p108 top right, p110 bottom middle.

Arthur Rothstein/CORBIS p35 bottom right

Jane Burton (image of dog on cover).

All other photographs and illustrations are the copyright of Quarto Publishing plc. While every effort has been made to credit contributors, Quarto would like to apologize should there have been any omissions or errors.

AUTHOR'S ACKNOWLEDGEMENTS

Special thanks to Dr. Rupert Sheldrake, and his research assistant Pamela Smart for all their help and encouragement in the research for this book.

Thanks also to Helena Zaugg Wildi, Herbert J. Rebhan, Elizabeth Bryan, and Lori Krug for their kind assistance in sharing their remarkable experiences with pets.